C000129296

Colin Bord was born in L......................................l
photographer and writer. Jar...............................a
freelance publisher's editor,.............................t
through their mutual intere.............................,
and now run a photo library............................d
rural Britain. Among other books they have written together are
Mysterious Britain, *The Secret Country* and *A Guide to Ancient Sites in
Britain*, all of which have been published in Paladin.

JANET AND COLIN BORD

Earth Rites

Fertility Practices in Pre-Industrial Britain

A PALADIN BOOK

GRANADA

London Toronto Sydney New York

Published in paperback by Granada Publishing Limited in 1983

ISBN 0 586 08452 5

First published in Great Britain by
Granada Publishing 1982

Granada Publishing Limited
Frogmore, St Albans, Herts AL2 2NF
and
36 Golden Square, London W1R 4AH
515 Madison Avenue, New York, NY 10022, USA
117 York Street, Sydney, NSW 2000, Australia
60 International Blvd, Rexdale, Ontario, R9W 6J2, Canada
61 Beach Road, Auckland, New Zealand

Printed and bound in Great Britain by
Hazell Watson & Viney Ltd,
Aylesbury, Bucks
Set in Plantin

Contents

Illustrations

About this book

Present-day materialism and the obsession with new technologies have tended to obscure mankind's true place in nature's cycle, and the proliferation in the West of diseases such as heart ailments and cancers is a clear sign that humanity is no longer living a natural, balanced life. The increasing urbanization, artificiality and pollution of life, mental and physical, have cut people off from what should be their natural heritage. Today we are all struggling for life, like plants without roots; and it is our empathy with the planet earth which we have lost.

The intention of *Earth Rites* is to indicate some of the ways in which our ancestors have been aware of the need to nurture the earth. For the continuance of life, it is vital that both man and earth are healthy and fruitful, and our predecessors evolved and successfully practised ways of maintaining fertility in man, beast and land. Their knowledge of and their interaction with their environment far exceeded ours, and today we can only guess at the methods they used, for all we have to study are a few artefacts of obscure meaning and degenerate customs and rituals now performed without knowledge of their original purpose.

A book of this size could not possibly cover the fertility practices of the whole world, and we have chosen to concentrate on Britain because that is where we live; but we have sometimes mentioned customs or artefacts from other countries to help emphasize a point. The British material is in many ways representative of what has been recorded in other parts of the world, but readers wishing for a wider view of the subject can consult the books listed in our bibliography.

As the twentieth century nears its end, there are positive signs that some people are beginning to rediscover humanity's dependence on a healthy planet. But far too many remain ignorant of these truths and the land continues to be slowly poisoned as, enamoured of the illusion of greater productivity and wealth, we vainly continue to despoil our heritage and lay the foundations for our forthcoming doom. But there is still time to retreat from the brink, and for a humble reappraisal of our way of life. We are not suggesting a return to a state of primitive agriculture, even if that were possible; but as a man thinks, so he acts, and if enough of the world's exploding population will seek to live in symbiosis with the planet there is hope for us yet. This book is our small attempt to show that there was an alternative lifestyle practised in the past and that its essence could be applied to our present precarious situation. Therefore we would like to dedicate this book to the Future.

1   The great Earth Mother

'You ask me to plough the ground? Shall I take a knife and tear my mother's bosom? Then when I die she will not take me to her bosom to rest. You ask me to dig for stone? Shall I dig under her skin for her bones? Then when I die I cannot enter her body to be born again. You ask me to cut grass and make hay and sell it, and be rich like white men! But how dare I cut off my mother's hair?'[1]

This outraged comment was made less than a hundred years ago by Smohalla, an American Indian prophet from the Umatilla tribe, but it echoes the past beliefs of people the world over. The earth was seen as a living body from which came all life, and to which all life returned. The survival and continuance of man, his crops and animals, was intimately bound up with the health of the Earth Mother, and man has always been careful to maintain the equilibrium of the life source. He may not always have been consciously aware of why he performed certain practices, and the traditional customs of the nineteenth and twentieth centuries are far removed from the essential rituals on which

The Earth as Nourishing Mother is depicted in this detail from an Exultet Roll illuminated at the Abbey of Monte Cassino, A.D. 1070–1100. Note the serpent, symbol of the life force and fertility.

1

they were based, but nevertheless there is still an instinctive if rarely verbalized knowledge of our close ties to the earth.

American-Indian creation myths tell how man came from deep inside the Earth Mother, after living and maturing for a while in her womb.[2] Such a belief may have once been worldwide, though it naturally took many forms, and many subsidiary beliefs developed. The Apache Indians saw the earth as their mother, facing upwards, and the sky as their father, facing downwards.[3] The sky god's semen took the form of rain which fertilized the earth. In both South Africa and Australia, women believed that they would become pregnant if they lay on the ground during a rain shower.[4] Agricultural communities saw the furrow in the soil as the earth's vulva, and the seeds they sowed as the semen.[5] In many civilizations, woman was identified with the furrow, the spade being the phallus.[6]

Water was not just the fertilizing element, not just the sky god's ejaculation. Terrestrial water sources were likened to a mother's nourishing breast milk, the most potent sources being wells and springs where pure water bubbled up out of the earth. In Britain and elsewhere such places were considered to be holy, and all manner of effects were attributed to the power in the water (see Chapter 6). Belief in the special qualities of sacred waters has persisted to the present day.

There are many other traces of belief in the earth as a living being. Some are slight, yet telling. Until early in the nineteenth century, the people of Tenby in Wales walked barefoot to church on Good Friday, so that they would not disturb the earth.[7] They may also have wished to make closer contact with the earth by removing their footwear. In some societies, the women would give birth directly on to the earth, or place the new-born baby on the ground as soon as possible after birth, as an acknowledgement of the child's true origins.[8] Unwanted children were sometimes left on the ground, for the Earth Mother to take care of.[9]

Beliefs such as these do not necessarily indicate that the primitive or 'natural' people who held them did not know the true 'facts of life'. On the contrary, their ability to live happy, healthy and fulfilled lives without needing twentieth-century 'necessities' shows that their knowledge of natural processes was deeper and more subtle than ours. Their belief in the Earth Mother was an acknowledgement of humanity's reliance on the earth, as their prime source of life. If we bear this in mind, we can see that apparently empty rituals performed to keep the earth fruitful may in fact have had a practical basis (see Chapter 12). Fertility charms like this one from Anglo-Saxon England may have been used to direct the speaker's vital energies on to one goal, and thus help bring about that goal.

> Erce, Erce, Erce, Earth Mother,
> may the Almighty Eternal Lord
> grant you fields to increase and flourish,
> fields fruitful and healthy,
> shining harvests of shafts of millet,
> broad harvests of barley ...
> Hail to thee, Earth, Mother of Men;
> Bring forth now in God's embrace,
> filled with good for the use of man.

Other appeals to the Earth Mother for assistance in agriculture will be found in Chapters 7 and 8, though some of these appeals, far removed from their origins, are hardly recognizable as such.

People who acknowledged the great Earth Mother naturally saw her body in their landscape. An obvious example of this is the naming of two breast-shaped hills in County Kerry as the Paps of Anu (a Celtic earth goddess). But long before the Celts named their earth goddess, early man saw his excursions deep into natural caves as a penetration into the body of the Earth Mother. Such places were special, and their importance was increased by the painting of animals, people, hunting scenes and indecipherable patterns and pictures on the cave walls. The

The Paps of Anu, County Kerry, seen as the breasts of the recumbent Earth Mother.

real meaning of these paintings is still unknown,[10] but some people think that these painted caves may have been creative ritual centres symbolizing the source of the animals hunted. In ancient times, mining had close parallels to terrestrial birth: the mines themselves were earth wombs, and the materials extracted were the embryos.[11] From Palaeolithic cave painters and prehistoric miners to the twentieth century is not long in terms of deep beliefs. In some Catholic countries prayers are offered to the Virgin Mary at grottoes, and where natural caves are used for this purpose there is a clear link with ancient practices. Also the Virgin Mary's role is evidently that of earth goddess or Earth Mother.

Mines and mine galleries were also seen as the earth's entrails (which in the mind of early man may have included the womb, as he may not have distinguished between the two).[12] Spiral and labyrinth designs can be interpreted as symbols of the earth's entrails, even as symbols of the Earth Mother herself,[13] and their worldwide use shows that they had a deep unconscious significance.[14] To some people the

Birth, death, rebirth; the eternal cycle; fertility and the generative life force: many aspects of life may have been symbolized by the triple spiral carved on stone C10 of the west side-chamber inside Newgrange passage-grave, County Meath.

4

spiral symbolized water and lunar fertility, and was carved on female idols,[15] while to others it symbolized the return to the Earth Mother at death. Spiral and labyrinthine carvings can be seen in a number of prehistoric burial chambers, and the famous triple spiral at Newgrange in County Meath may symbolize the cyclic nature of death and rebirth. Much later usages of the labyrinth idea in the form of mazes cut in the turf or built of stones may also have had a fertility significance, in that ritual dances or races through the mazes could have symbolized the rebirth of life at springtime. Documentary evidence is lacking, but May Eve games were certainly held at one turf maze, the 'Julian's Bower' at Alkborough, Humberside.

Natural landscape features have long been interpreted as parts of the Earth Mother's anatomy. The Paps of Anu, already mentioned, are the most famous of many examples of breast-shaped hills. The names of the hills often show where this feature has been noticed: 'toot' as in Toot Hill probably equates with 'teat', and *mam* in Welsh, a gently rising hill, may also have had the same meaning.[16] Wimble Toot, a tumulus near Babcary in Somerset, lies on the breast of the Virgo figure in the controversial Glastonbury zodiac, a collection of gigantic figures said to be outlined by natural and manmade features in the Somerset landscape.[17] Twin round barrows may also have been seen by their prehistoric builders as breasts and therefore as symbols of the Earth Mother. Glastonbury Tor, too, has been seen as a breast.[18] On top is a church tower: is it only coincidence that hill and tower together strongly resemble a breast and nipple? Or were the church builders consciously locating the church where it could perform a dual pagan and Christian role? At Llanbrynmair in Powys the church was built on the summit of a little hill and an old saying, 'Llanbrynmair llun bron merch', compares the shape to a woman's breast.[19]

There are numerous examples of how ancient man in Britain seems to have moulded the landscape in order to enhance its maternal qualities. With no written records left behind to guide us, our interpretation of what we see today is fallible, and one man's goddess is another man's chimera. With that warning in mind, let us describe some *possible* early attempts to delineate the body of the Earth Mother. We shall here deal only with earth structures and composite stone structures such as tombs. Standing stones as phallic symbols and holed stones as female symbols will be discussed and illustrated in Chapter 4.

Breasts in the landscape: Wimble Toot (above); a tumulus and bell barrow at Winterbourne Stoke crossroads in Wiltshire (top right); and Glastonbury Tor (bottom right).

The whole body of the Earth Mother or goddess is rarely identified, but Michael Dames believes he has found such a goddess centring on Silbury Hill in Wiltshire, where twenty-seven Neolithic monuments such as long barrows, causewayed camps and stone circles, together with the natural features and contours of the landscape, form a '33-mile topographic image'.[20] Dames has also devoted considerable effort to solving the riddle of Silbury Hill, a mysterious earth mound 130 feet high, built by prehistoric man around 2500 BC for purposes unknown. Archaeological excavations, the latest in 1968-70, have failed to discover any traces of a burial, so it seems unlikely that this magnificent earth-moving feat was undertaken in order to construct a tomb for an important figure. Dames sees the hill and its encircling moat as 'the Great Goddess in her pregnant state', giving birth annually at Lammas when harvest begins.[21] Other writers have also noted the womb-like appearance of certain artificial conical mounds,[22] and another Wiltshire example is Old Sarum just outside Salisbury. This is an oval, flat-topped hill surrounded by the deep ditch of the

Silbury Hill is often surrounded by water, and it is thought that this was the intention of its Neolithic builders. Michael Dames sees Silbury as a 'primordial hill' rising from the waters.

original Iron Age hillfort. Its extent is over twenty-five acres, and its uterine shape and appearance, protected by the rampart and ditch, have been appreciated by later occupiers of the site, for a Norman castle there was followed by a mediaeval cathedral, the outline of which still remains. The 'Mother Church' as 'creative and regenerative' is symbolized in this choice of site.[23]

The uterine earth circle of Old Sarum.

Just as earth mounds projecting above the earth have been seen as representing the Earth Mother's body or womb, so too have rooms and tunnels dug into the earth been interpreted in the same way. In some parts of Britain, notably Cornwall, Scotland and Ireland, underground chambers associated with ancient pre-Roman settlements have been found. Called fogous, souterrains or earth-houses, they are stone-lined passages of varying length, sometimes with side passages or chambers. Conventionally described as food stores or hiding places, they may also, or instead, have been constructed with the intention of forming an entrance into the body of the Earth Mother. An important feature of American Indian settlements was the kiva ('world below'). This was a large chamber (usually underground) which developed from the earliest Indian pit houses, storage pits and burial pits. Seen as a womb or entrance into the Earth Mother's body, the kiva was entered through a hole in the roof, and there was a small hole in the floor symbolizing the route into the underworld. Many sacred ceremonies were performed in the kiva, which was the settlement's focal point.[24] It seems possible that the British fogou could, at least as a part of its use, have been a similar structure to the kiva.

Womb-like stone structures were also built above ground throughout western Europe, though they are now more usually identified strictly as tombs. It is true that they were used in that way, as places to house the corpses or cremated remains of the dead, but some authorities suggest that the tomb symbolized the Earth Mother's womb, in which the dead rested until reborn. Right back to the earliest times there are hints that man believed in rebirth. Archaeologists have found evidence that Palaeolithic man placed corpses in a crouched or foetal position, and also sometimes painted them with red ochre, perhaps as a symbol of the life-blood.[25] Animal sacrifices sometimes accompanied the burial, as if it was intended to leave the dead person food for his future use.[26] Cremation was thought of as a return to the seed state; and in India the Hindus used to mix actual seeds with cremated human remains and sprinkle the mixture over freshly ploughed fields, saying 'May Sāvitrī sprinkle thy flesh in the bosom of our mother the Earth.'[27]

The structure of some stone tombs does suggest a womb: a long, low, narrow passage (the vagina) leads to a chamber deep within the earth mound (the womb or uterus). Inside some tombs are phallic pillars, or stones carved as goddess figures (see Chapter 4), as if to

Inside Halliggye fogou, Mawgan-in-Meneage, Cornwall.

The Animal Room, a kiva at the pueblo of Zuni, New Mexico, photographed in 1899.

Bryn-Celli-Ddu burial chamber on the island of Anglesey, Gwynedd:
looking into the entrance (top), and inside the passage, looking towards
the central chamber.

reinforce the womb/tomb symbolism. The structures known as dolmens appear to have had a special significance. Dolmens (or quoits or cromlechs) are found today principally in Ireland, Wales and Cornwall, and consist of large upright stones topped by a capstone. Sometimes very slight traces of an earth mound have been located, and archaeologists believe that originally the stones were covered with earth and used as tombs. Perhaps they were; but they probably also had other uses. It is interesting that dolmens are also found on the Melanesian island of Malekula in the New Hebrides. Their name for the structure means 'to come out from, to be born',[28] and the dolmen symbolizes 'a stone grave, the cave through which the dead must pass on their journey to the other world, and the womb through which the living may achieve rebirth.'[29] So as well as being the womb from which the dead are reborn, the dolmen is also used in ceremonies in which the living experience a rebirth, as in initiation at puberty. It is likely that dolmens in western Europe were used in the same way. In fact it is even possible that they were built as we now see them, and never were covered with earth.

There are other ancient stone structures which later researchers

Lanyon Quoit, Cornwall.

have seen as symbolizing the body of the goddess or Earth Mother. The ground plans of Neolithic temples in Malta suggest the female body, as do the shapes of some Neolithic dwellings on Orkney, Shetland, and elsewhere.[30]

If today's researchers are correct in their interpretation of the evidence, it does seem that early man constructed symbolic stone wombs within which vital rituals could be performed, with the understanding that the life and wellbeing of the people was thereby enhanced. Nor did the belief in an Earth Mother disappear with the passage of time. It found expression in a multiplicity of goddesses around the world, all of them involved in the continuation of life and fertility. There was, for example, the Greek goddess Gaea, Gaia or Ge; the Roman earth-goddess and goddess of fecundity Tellus Mater; Frey, a Scandinavian god of plenty and fertility; the Slavonic 'Moist Mother Earth', Mati-Syra-Zemlya; the Finno-Ugric Mother of Mannu, earth divinity; and the earth and mother goddess of the Aztecs in South America, Coatlicue.[31]

In Britain it was the Celts who worshipped fertility goddesses, the main names we know today being Macha, Danu/Anu, Brigit/Brigid/Bride. The evidence is both complex and confusing, and we have no room to trace the history of these goddesses.

The basic Celtic goddess type was at once mother, warrior, hag, virgin, conveyor of fertility, of strong sexual appetite which led her to seek mates amongst mankind equally with the gods, giver of prosperity to the land, protectress of the flocks and herds. More static and more archaic than the gods, she remained tied to the land for which she was responsible and whose most striking natural features seemed to her worshippers to be manifestations of her power and personality.[32]

This quotation from Dr Anne Ross's *Pagan Celtic Britain* encapsulates the many attributes of the Celtic goddesses, and we will concentrate here on the surviving fertility aspects of their worship. The name 'Macha' describes three war-fertility goddesses,[33] while Anu and Danu may have been the same person. 'They' were the 'divine mother of early Irish mythology'[34] and gave their name to the County Kerry mountains, the Paps of Anu. Brigit or Brigid was another triple goddess, who became the Christian St Brigid/Brigit/Bridget/Bride, and was widely worshipped in Scotland and Ireland. In the Scottish Highlands women in labour sought Bride's help in bringing about an easy delivery. She also brought life to the dead winter, and her day was

14

1 February, which was when the ancient pagan Celtic festival of Imbolc was held.

On the eve of St Bride's Day, girls used to make and decorate corn dollies which they took to each household. Everyone had to give a

A straw brideóg from Ballycreggan, Kiltoom, Athlone, County Roscommon.

small present to Bride, and special cakes were baked. After a procession the girls celebrated with feasting and dancing. The older women made straw cradles or baskets called Bride's Bed. An image of Bride made of oats was placed inside and a wooden wand was given to her. If next morning the marks of this wand could be seen in the ashes on the hearth, that was a good omen for the coming year.[35] In Ireland, the Brideóg, a small straw doll, was dressed up and taken from door to door on St Bridget's Eve; Bridget's Crosses made of rushes were placed on the buildings to guard against evil spirits; and a protective charm in the form of a straw rope with crosses on it, a Bridget's Girdle, was worn on St Bridget's Day itself. In some parts a rush or twig bed was made by the fire so that the saint could rest there.[36]

Bride's importance as a fertility goddess is indicated in another traditional Scottish belief: that on St Bride's Day a serpent came out of the hill. One version of a hymn sung to it was:

> Early on Bride's morn
> The serpent shall come from the hole,
> I will not molest the serpent,
> Nor will the serpent molest me.[37]

If the serpent symbolizes earth energy, as we suggest in Chapter 12, the meaning of this song becomes clearer. The surviving evidence does suggest that in the earliest times, before the rituals were handed down from one generation to the next and became garbled and incomprehensible, there was a universal knowledge of how the earth's fertility could and should be maintained.

Belief in earth goddesses was a long time dying, and one late survival was the festival of Blaeberry Sunday when people used to visit a rocky hillock in County Armagh known as Cailleach Bhéara's Chair. Cailleach Bhéara herself was believed to live under a cairn on top of the hill.[38] Today we are rational people and no longer believe in the old goddesses (who have now been turned into saints), but still we have a tendency to anthropomorphize nature, and to see human heads and forms in rock formations, on trees, in clouds, on insects and plants.[39] Can we still be dreaming of the days when we *knew* that we lived on the body of the great Earth Mother?

2 The archaeological evidence for fertility cults

'Crawl to your Mother Earth. She will save you from the void.'

Rigveda, XVIII, 10

The further back in time we go, the more enigmatic becomes the evidence for fertility practices. We have all kinds of hints and clues, but little tangible evidence. There are no written records, and most of the prehistoric rock carvings and paintings have no obvious meaning to twentieth-century man. Scholars have pieced together the fragments of evidence and have come to the conclusion that fertility cults were widespread in prehistoric times,[1] and in this chapter we will look at just one aspect of the evidence: artefacts discovered in archaeological explorations.

Beginning with the earliest, we must go right back to the Upper Palaeolithic or Old Stone Age, which began around 40,000 BC. It was during this time that the cave artists were active in Europe, leaving on inaccessible cave walls thousands of paintings of beasts, people and symbols, including what appear to be vulvas. Some interpreters believe that the paintings were used in sympathetic magic, perhaps to increase the fertility and therefore the numbers of animals available for food.[2] The cave artists also made sculptures, some of them female figures now known collectively as 'Venus figurines' because of their shape and their supposed erotic nature. The best-known ones are the Venus of Laussel (found at Marquay in the Dordogne, France), the Venus of Willendorf (found at Willendorf, Wachau, Lower Austria) and the Venus of Věstonice (found at Dolní Věstonice, Moravia, Czechoslovakia). The figures are small (the Willendorf Venus is about $4\frac{1}{2}$ inches high and carved in limestone) and show mature women with their sexual characteristics emphasized. Some people see them as representing mother goddesses, and this seems a likely interpretation. Erich Neumann succinctly describes them thus in his study of the Great Mother:

The unshapely figures of the Great Mother are representations of the pregnant goddess of fertility, who was looked upon throughout the world as

Three 'Venus figurines': the Věstonice Venus (top left), the Willendorf Venus (top right), and the Laussel Venus (bottom left). The cornucopia or Horn of Plenty held by the Laussel Venus symbolizes abundance and fertility, as well as being both phallic (horn-shaped) and feminine (hollow and receptive).

The chalk statuette found at Grimes Graves (bottom right).

the goddess of pregnancy and childbearing, and who, as a cult object not only of women but also of men, represents the archetypal symbol of fertility and of the sheltering, protecting, and nourishing elementary character.[3]

However, this is not the only possibility, and archaeologist Evan Hadingham, who has studied Palaeolithic art, is one who does not support it. Instead he wonders, 'Could they just be amulets to bring good luck?'[4]

In Britain the nearest artefact to a 'Venus figurine' so far discovered is the chalk 'goddess' from Grimes Graves in Norfolk. Today deep hollows in the wild breckland show the site of the Neolithic flint mines which were in use between 3000 and 2500 BC. Over 360 filled-in mine shafts have been found, and one of them, thirty feet deep, is open to the public. In another pit close by the miners left a chalk statuette with a chalk phallus and a pile of flint nodules and antler picks in front of it. The phallus and the pregnant woman suggest that the miners were trying to stimulate the Earth Mother into producing the 'offspring' they most desired at that place, flint. Apparently that particular mine was deficient, and was abandoned shortly after the statuette was set up.[5]

Chalk phalli have been found at other prehistoric sites in Britain, suggesting that some kind of fertility cult was practised. Rites and ceremonies for fertility purposes were probably one of the reasons why such sites as Windmill Hill causewayed camp in Wiltshire and Maumbury Rings henge in Dorset were constructed. Evidence for the nature of their use is sparse, but the fact that they were large sites suitable for gatherings, and that chalk phalli were found there, does suggest that ritual fertility ceremonies took place. Phalli have also been found in burial mounds, such as Winterbourne Stoke long barrow on Salisbury Plain in Wiltshire and Thickthorn long barrow in Dorset. A link between death and renewal of life is suggested, reminiscent of the themes in Chapter 1. Chalk figures have also been found, or at least these crude chalk objects have been interpreted as figures. Most lack heads and arms, but do have a deep vertical groove between where the thighs might be. The example from Maiden Castle hillfort in Dorset, illustrated here, shows how basic these figures are, and it may be possible that twentieth-century interpreters are reading into them what was not intended. They certainly bear no relationship to the 'Venus figurines' or Grimes Grave goddess whose connection with fertility seems clearly stated. A similar chalk figurine was also

Romano-British phallic amulet found in Dorset (top).
Phallic head from Eype, Dorset (bottom left). For the Celts the severed
head was a powerful symbol of the life-force, and in Celtic art the head
and phallus were often combined.
Chalk figure found at Maiden Castle (bottom right).

found at Windmill Hill, the location too of thirty small chalk balls found in pairs and possibly intended to represent male organs.

Figures were carved from chalk where it was plentiful. Elsewhere, wood was used, and the natural decay of this substance has meant that wooden fertility figures are rare. One intriguing figure dating back to the Neolithic period survived in Somerset, where it was recovered in 1966 from the Bell trackway. The 6-inch ashwood figure, called the

Two wooden figures thought to date from around the sixth century B.C. That on the left is 3 feet 9 inches high and was found in a bog near Shercock in County Cavan. The other figure, from Dagenham, is 1 foot 6 inches high.

'God-dolly' by its excavators, is a hermaphrodite with breasts and phallus, and seems to have been placed in position during the building of the track.[6] Phallic wooden figures dating from the late Bronze Age or early Iron Age have also been found, in a well preserved state. The phallus was separate, each body having a hole for the insertion of this organ. This hole could also, of course, be interpreted as a female vagina, but the figures have no breasts. The figure from Dagenham was made of pinewood which indicates its prehistoric origin since the pine early became extinct in England. A wooden female figure was found at Ballachulish in Argyll, Scotland, having been preserved in the peat since the early Celtic period. She had clear sexual organs, and frightening facial features, the eyes inlaid with pebbles.[7] Well-preserved wooden gods and goddesses found in Danish bogs show the kind of carvings that probably existed in Britain but have been lost through decay.[8]

All the carved figures are small when compared with the 180-foot rampantly male figure emblazoned on a hill at Cerne Abbas in Dorset. The 'Cerne giant', naked and carrying a club, was probably cut into the chalk at the end of the second century AD, in the 'Romano-British period', and so is later than the wooden figures just described. He may

The 30-foot phallus of the Cerne Abbas Giant.

This small (10.5 inches high) 'mother goddess' carving was found in Gwent at Caerwent, which was the Roman Venta Silurum. There is some evidence for a healing cult at a shrine there. The carving, dating from the first to fourth centuries A.D., is Celtic in appearance, unlike the Roman-looking goddesses illustrated overleaf.

have been part of Emperor Commodius' plan to revive the cult of Hercules.[9] A carving (called 'Hercules' by Anne Ross) of a naked man brandishing a club, and looking very similar to the Cerne giant, was found at the Roman site of Corstopitum (Corbridge) in Northumberland.[10] The Cerne giant may have formed part of a fertility cult. As

This trio of goddesses shows how the Romans often honoured 'the mothers' or 'Matres'. They hold fruits and other foodstuffs, and clearly symbolize the fertility of the earth. This stone relief was found at Cirencester in Gloucestershire, which as Corinium Dobunnorum was the second largest town after London in Roman Britain.

we shall see in Chapter 3, both the giant and an earthwork above him were involved in fertility practices until fairly recently.

The worship of mother goddesses was mentioned in Chapter 1, and this is one aspect of fertility cults for which archaeologists have been able to find reliable physical evidence. When the Romans invaded

The Celtic goddess Brigantia in Roman dress. 3 feet high, the figure dates from the second or third century A.D. When translated the inscription reads: *Sacred to Brigantia: Amandus, the engineer, fulfilled the order by command.*

Britain they brought their own religious beliefs and practices with them, and they also seem to have absorbed some Celtic gods and goddesses into their pantheon. The Romans seemed to need little excuse to indulge in stone carving, judging from the number of such carvings that have survived, with the result that there is plenty of

A small carving of a mother goddess in the Roman Temple of Mithras at Carrawburgh in Northumberland.

surviving evidence for their religious practices, even if such evidence is not easy to interpret. Mother goddess carvings are frequent, their nature being shown by the cornucopias, fruit, bread, and babies which accompany them. Goddesses often appear in threes, which demonstrates the 'fundamental Celtic belief in the threefold power of the divinity',[11] but there are also many single goddesses depicted in carvings, such as the stone relief of Brigantia (illustrated p. 25) which was found at the Roman fort of Blatobulgium (Birrens) in Dumfriesshire. The Brigantes were a tribe living in northern England, but this carving suggests that they also occupied the south-west corner of Scotland. Brigantia was their deity, her name meaning 'High One' or 'Queen', and she is probably the same goddess as Brigid or Bride whom we met in Chapter 1. The finding of this carving at a Roman fort illustrates how the imported and native traditions blended.[12]

This same theme is illustrated by the numerous face-pots, artefacts from Roman Britain but with Celtic associations. They are urns decorated with crude human faces, and sometimes what looks like a phallus can be seen below the head. The head was an important religious symbol to the Celts, and we shall discuss their head-cult later in this book. Also it was often associated with the phallus, as shown in the small phallic head illustrated earlier in this chapter, and this has led archaeologists to believe that the face-pots were probably associated with fertility and burial rites.[13]

The carvings we have just described date from around 1,700 years ago, and even though the interpretation of this evidence is complicated, the Romano-British tradition seems positively simple and straightforward to understand when compared with the relics of our Late Stone Age (Neolithic) predecessors of 4,000–7,000 years ago. Those Stone Age peoples also left carvings behind, but interpretation of them has so far proved impossible.[14] In Chapter 1 we have already considered how carved spirals can be seen as symbols of death and rebirth, an interpretation accepted by many researchers. One archaeologist who plunged into the muddy waters and came out with a revolutionary new theory to account for some of the carvings was Dr O. G. S. Crawford, founder and editor of *Antiquity* magazine. In his book *The Eye Goddess*[15] he describes the cult of an Eye Goddess, an agricultural fertility cult which spread westwards and northwards from Syria, and in Britain is evidenced by rock carvings of faces and eyes. Like many before and since, Dr Crawford has tried hard to find some meaning in the enigmatic circles, cups and squiggles left on the stones of Neolithic burial chambers and elsewhere, especially in western Scotland and Ireland. (Ronald Morris lists *104* possible interpretations in his book on Galloway rock art.)[16] But so far as eyes or faces are concerned, it should be realized that these carvings are such that if you are looking for eyes and faces, you will certainly find them. That does not mean that the carvers intended to depict eyes and faces. So whether Dr Crawford was right, and these carvings were part of a fertility cult, must remain unproven for the time being.

So we see that archaeologists have found a little evidence for ancient fertility cults, the evidence being more enigmatic the further back in time it comes from. But can anything be read from the evidence? Archaeologist Aubrey Burl suggests in *Prehistoric Avebury* that ancient man did indulge in ceremonies, probably involving sexual

The faces described by Dr Crawford are often difficult to see, but carvings on chalk cylinders found in a child's grave at Folkton Wold in North Yorkshire are clearly intended to represent faces. The three cylinders are 3.5 inches high and 4 inches in diameter, and date from around 1800–1500 B.C. This early interest in the head suggests that the head-cult actually pre-dated the Celts who are usually associated with it.

intercourse, to stimulate the fertility of earth and man. He supports his theory by introducing evidence from Scandinavia, including a carved stone from Maltegaard (illustrated in our Chapter 8) which is described by Danish archaeologist Dr P. V. Glob as a 'cult-disc'.[17] The Bronze Age carving depicts a man with erect penis reaching out to a woman, and between them is a hole in the stone possibly symbolizing the earth. Many Scandinavian rock carvings also show copulation and other sexual activity in a ritual setting, thus indicating the existence of fertility cults.[18]

If archaeological discoveries give us hints of ancient fertility practices, perhaps folklore will supply a clearer picture.

3 Fertility in folklore

'In fertility and generation, woman does not set an example to the earth, but the earth sets an example to woman.'

Plato, *Menexenus*

The belief that the Earth's vital energies could be used to maintain the fertility of the people survived in customs which have spanned the centuries from prehistoric times to the last century, and even persist to the present day in certain degenerate forms. Standing stones, which are firmly anchored down into the earth and therefore act as a focus for the Earth Mother's energies, were frequently visited and rituals performed with the expectation of ensuring fertility or curing barrenness. Earlier in the marital sequence, couples visited certain holed stones to seal their betrothal as at Tresco in the Scilly Isles, where in the old abbey gardens was a stone with two holes. Engaged couples would grasp each other's hands through the holes and so plight their troth. Young men and women would exchange their betrothal vows within the stone circle at Callanish on the island of Lewis off the north-west coast of Scotland. The circle was also apparently an auspicious place to consummate a marriage.[1] The Stone of Odin, a holed stone now destroyed but formerly standing near the Stones of Stenness on Orkney mainland, was visited by couples who had first gone to the Stenness Stones and to the Ring of Brodgar to begin their betrothal. They would clasp right hands through the hole in the Stone of Odin, and swear to be faithful.[2] At Lairg in Sutherland there was a 'Plightin' Stane' built into the church wall (now demolished) used for making pledges, including the sealing of betrothals,[3] while in County Antrim in Northern Ireland the holed stone near Doagh was visited to ratify marriage contracts, again by the couple clasping hands through the hole.[4]

In some places actual marriages were performed at holed stones, for example at Kirk Braddan on the Isle of Man where there are stone rings in the churchyard. During the wedding ceremony, the couple would clasp hands through the hole in one of these stones. At Kilchouslan in Kintyre (Strathclyde), eloping couples were regarded as lawfully married after they had clasped hands through a holed

The holed stone near Doagh.

At Trethevy Quoit in Cornwall is a clear example of a stone with a section cut away, presumably to allow a way into the tomb.

stone.[5] Archaeologist Aubrey Burl sees a parallel between the custom of clasping hands through a holed stone and the use in prehistoric times of stones with holes cut into them as doorways into megalithic tombs. The bones of the dead were passed through the hole, which signified the entry into another world, and, presumably, the first step towards a new life, as did the hand-clasping to the betrothing couples.[6]

The linking of wedding celebrations with ancient sites in folklore and custom echoes the ritual dances that were once presumably held at such sites, and the belief that the sites were somehow involved in maintaining fertility. On Colonsay, an island off the west coast of Scotland, marriages took place at Sithean Mor (the large fairy knowe) until the early nineteenth century.[7] In some places, notably the Shropshire/Wales border[8] and on the Welsh coast near Harlech,[9] gunpowder was traditionally fired at certain stones to celebrate a wedding, the gunpowder being detonated in holes made in the stone. As well as linking the wedding ceremony to the Earth, this custom could also be a dim memory of fire rituals. Legends of weddings at ancient sites persist too, the most famous one in Britain being at Stanton Drew in Avon. Here, the remains of three stone circles are said to be the petrified members of a wedding party who danced on the Sabbath to music provided by the Devil.[10] There are a number of sites with a similar legend in France,[11] while stones in Gambia and Peshawar (Pakistan) are also said to be petrified wedding parties.[12]

Certain sites were traditionally resorted to directly for fertility purposes, some to ensure fertility, others to cure barrenness. Newly married couples would hold hands and walk round the Kempock Stane near Gourock in Strathclyde, asking for a fruitful union,[13] while the Tolven Stone near Helford in Cornwall ensured fertility if the naked petitioner squeezed through it.[14] It was the dew that collected on top of the Magic Stone of Southery in Norfolk which held its potency, according to an old man of eighty who claimed that he was still fertile because he drank the dew every morning.[15]

Childless women would visit stones such as the holed stone at Glencolumkille in County Donegal where they would pray for offspring,[16] or the Kelpie Stane in the River Dee near Dinnet (Grampian), where they passed through a hole in the stone in the same direction as the stream,[17] or King's Park in Edinburgh where they would slide along a recumbent stone.[18] Also in Scotland, barren women would hope to become fertile by sitting on a certain stone in Brahan Wood near Dingwall (Highland),[19] or in artificial rock basins

A detail of the west side of the shaft of the cross at Boho. The worn carvings of the late ninth or early tenth century include a depiction of Adam and Eve with the tree and serpent.

in a shelving rock on the Loch Avon side of Cairngorm.[20] It was childless men who visited the cross at Boho near Enniskillen in County Fermanagh.[21] Country people also sometimes sought cures for barren livestock. In County Cork a barren sow could be cured if a

On the island of Inishmurray off the west coast of Ireland, there are two cross-slabs outside Teampull-na-mBan (Women's Church) which were used to ensure easy birth, and the nearer slab in the photograph is one of them. The pregnant woman would kneel on the ground and place her fingers in the side holes and thumbs in two holes below the cross, and then haul herself upright.

healer touched it through the hole in a stone at Caherurlagh.[22]

Those women lucky enough not to need to resort to a stone to cure barrenness might still go to one to ensure easy childbirth. At Clocnapeacaib in County Cork they would draw articles of their clothing through the holed stone, [23] while pregnant women would perform a ritual round the White Lady of Ballafreer, a quartz pillar on the Isle of Man.[24]

Of course practices such as these were not confined to the British Isles. People in many other parts of the world believed in the power of their own fertilizing stones, for example India, Australia, New Guinea, Madagascar, Africa, and especially France, where many examples have been recorded.[25] In northern California, USA, certain carved boulders in the Pomo territory were known as 'baby rocks', and ceremonies performed there by women wishing for children.[26]

Why should people down the ages and all over the world have had such faith in standing stones? Was it simply the phallic shape of many of the stones, which caused the desperate women to see them as active symbols of the fertility they so longed for? Mircea Eliade, a scholar who has made a lifelong study of comparative religion and has written widely on folklore and its meaning, suggests that the phallic symbolism of the standing stone is not at all the main reason for its importance as a source of fertility. He sees standing stones as part of a prehistoric 'cult of the dead', and suggests that 'In all probability, these stones constituted a sort of "substitute body", in which the souls of the dead were incorporated. In the last analysis, *a stone "substitute" was a body built for eternity.*' Therefore the standing stones, representing the dead ancestors, would hold 'an inexhaustible reservoir of vitality and power', and this is what the later peoples hoped to tap when they visited the stones, touched them, sat upon them, rubbed against them, and slid down them.[27]

Professor Eliade's explanation does not allow for any physical basis to the fertility beliefs. Unfortunately no one seems to have carried out any experiments to ascertain whether barren women have become fertile as a result of resorting to so-called fertility stones. But it is not impossible that the beliefs did have a factual basis. Stan Gooch suggests that negative ions were generated at ancient sites, and mentions that negative ions are known to 'have an influence in respect of sexuality and fertility'.[28] In Chapter 12 we discuss the possible use of standing stones as focuses for or collectors of an energy, the nature of which we are as yet uncertain of, and the research being done to find out more about this energy and its behaviour. Although the evidence for the existence of this energy is still tenuous, *evidence there is*, and dowsers have had a large part to play in locating it. Although most people have some dowsing ability, few have nurtured it. Practising dowsers have a well developed sensitivity to emanations and radiations, and no doubt there have always been such people who were able to trace invisible energies. We may now only possess the barest knowledge of an ancient system of earth and cosmic energies which was once well understood and utilized, one of its values being its power to restore fertility to the body. Although all real knowledge of the vitalizing energy was gradually forgotten, the rituals were still followed, and the belief in their efficacy continued.

Not only stones artificially placed by man were visited to promote fertility. Some other sites such as certain natural rock outcrops were also considered efficacious. In the light of the idea that ancient people were sensitive to subtle energy currents, that they could identify where the currents were strongest, and knew how to channel and utilize them, it is logical to suggest that sometimes sites other than standing stones should be associated with fertility, and that the necessary energies could also accumulate at sites where it was perhaps not possible or necessary to erect a standing stone to focus and dispense the energy. The Stone of the Woman (Clach-na-Bhan) in Grampian is one such site, a granite rock on top of the hill Meall-Ghaineah in Glen Avon near Braemar. Here women would sit to secure husbands, and later they would return to achieve a painless childbirth.[29] A similar site was the Bride's Chair at Warton in Lancashire, a seat-like hollow in a crag. A girl who sat in the chair on her wedding day would certainly have a family.[30] In Ireland, a married woman without children might have resorted to spending the night in a cleft in the rock at the source of the River Lee.[31] So-called 'saints' beds' were common in Ireland, and some of them had reputations for curing barrenness. The 'beds' were holes in the ground or hollows in rocks, and in about 1873 the Reverend James Page described the ritual associated with St Patrick's Bed on Croagh Patrick, the holy mountain in County Mayo.

All the devotees do not go there – none but those that are barren – and the abominable practices committed there ought to make human nature, in its most degraded state, blush. This station course is forty yards in circumference. Round this they go seven times, then enter the bed, turn round seven times, take up some small pebbles, and bring them home, in order to prevent barrenness, and to banish rats and mice. The greater part of those who go through this station stop upon the hill all night that they may sleep in the bed.[32]

In cases where it was the custom to follow a ritual involving lying on the earth or in a rock hollow, the practice may have stemmed from an instinctive desire to be as close as possible to the Earth Mother, and to invoke her aid in the restoration of fertility. In some rural communities where the cottages had earth floors, it was customary for a woman in 'childbed' to lie directly on the earth, 'so that she might draw strength from the earth whence she and all men sprang'.[33]

Over the centuries, other sites and objects, sometimes linked to the earth and sometimes not, have been credited with the ability to promote fertility, and so we will describe a few of the more interesting examples. One earth site with obvious strong fertility connections is the Cerne Abbas Giant in Dorset. It is hardly surprising that this chalk hill figure, already briefly mentioned in Chapter 2, should have been regarded as a potent source of fertility. Barren women sat on the figure, presumably on the phallus itself as being the most relevant part

The Cerne Abbas Giant.

of the giant's anatomy, though some people believed that in order to cure barrenness, the man and woman should have sexual intercourse on the giant. In the photograph can be seen a small earth enclosure above the giant's head. This was known as the Frying Pan, and on 30 April a firwood maypole used to be erected annually, ready for the May Day festivities.[34] As later chapters will illustrate, such celebrations were originally fertility rituals, and the maypole itself can be thought of as a giant phallus.

An old oak chair in St Paul's church, Jarrow (Tyne and Wear), was another well-known fertility site. The chair is thought to have been that of the Venerable Bede (673–735), the historian and scholar who lived and died at Jarrow. Brides believed that to sit in the chair immediately after the wedding ceremony would bring them children, and pregnant women drank water in which small pieces of wood from the chair had been soaked, in order to ensure a pain-free childbirth.[35] Another church fertility site is at Ashingdon in Essex, where in mediaeval times there was a shrine which was said to ensure fertility if visited. Although the shrine no longer exists, Ashingdon church kept a reputation as a lucky place to get married.[36] In Scotland, a practice recorded at Burghead in Grampian is probably the remnants of a fertility custom. Children would use a stone to strike a wall-mounted memorial stone in the Chapel Yard cemetery, and then claimed to hear the sound of a rocking cradle and crying child. Thus the stone became known as the Cradle Stone. In the eighteenth century women who heard these sounds believed they would become pregnant.[37]

A number of holy wells were considered to be able to bestow fertility on women, and we shall investigate these in Chapter 6. One Scottish fertility custom involved both stone and water. In Sandsting parish, Shetland, a quartz pebble the shape and size of an egg was placed in water drawn from a running stream, and the woman who wished for children washed her feet in the water.[38] Also to be discussed in more detail later (see Chapter 5) are the small carvings of women with exposed genitals commonly known as sheela-na-gigs, and usually found at old churches, both in Britain and Ireland. Some of these may have been involved in fertility rituals, or thought of as sources of fertility.

Country people also used to practise traditional customs which were intended to ensure personal fertility, as in North Uist, off the north-west coast of Scotland, where on 28 September Carrot Sunday was celebrated. The women and girls went out and gathered certain

Bede's Chair, Jarrow.

types of wild carrot, singing a special song:

> Cleft fruitful, fruitful, fruitful,
> Joy of carrots surpassing upon me,
> Michael the brave endowing me,
> Bride the fair be aiding me;
> Progeny pre-eminent over every progeny,
> Progeny on my womb, progeny on my progeny,
> Progeny pre-eminent over every progeny.

(Note the reference to Bride, fertility goddess whom we met in Chapter 1.)

Forked carrots were especially prized as a fertility symbol. On the next day, St Michael's Day, the women gave to each other and to the men bunches of carrots, and were wished 'Children and blessings upon you' in return, or a similar good wish. This was only a part of the St Michael's Day celebrations, which involved much revelry and dancing.[39]

Another fertility custom was the throwing of nuts at a wedding, now superseded by confetti-throwing which has the same meaning – to promote fertility. Nuts used to be known as a symbol of fertility, and a good nut crop signified plenty of births during the following year.[40] In Yorkshire, a virgin about to marry at harvest-time would secretly go to a cornfield and collect straws from the stooks – one wheat straw for each boy child she wished for, and one oat straw for each girl. She made a garter of them, reciting the correct words as she did so, and wore it round her leg. If it stayed in place from Friday evening (when she should make it) until the following Monday morning, all would be well, but if it broke, the charm would not work. Also, only a virgin could use this charm. Its use would bring evil to the children of a lapsed virgin.[41]

Although today the straw garter has been superseded by the fertility drug, we should not imagine that some women are not still inclined to follow old fertility practices, or to invent new ones. In some parts of the world it seems that unusual (to the local population) objects are bestowed with an aura of mystery and strange powers attributed to them. During the advance of the Egyptian army on Khartoum in 1898, W. T. Maud who was a *Graphic* artist wrote:

The natives look upon the engine as a sort of god, and stand in awe of it. The sapper officers who built the line, have many amusing yarns to tell about their reception when first the locomotive came along. At Gennanetti, an Arab approached the officer in charge, and asked him if his wife might creep under the engine. The reason for this extraordinary request, was that the lady was anxious to have a child, so permission was at once given. Not content with crawling under the engine once, she asked if she might do it again, and her husband explained that this would ensure her having twins.[42]

A shower of confetti symbolizes the guests' unspoken hopes for a fruitful marriage.

At Paestum in Italy in 1973, women were visiting the Roman temple ruins and sitting astride a certain stone which had acquired a reputation as a fertility stone,[43] while in Dallas, Texas, in 1976 women were flocking to the public library to borrow a wooden doll which women from the Ashanti tribe had carried on their backs if they wished to become pregnant. It was said that several Dallas women had become pregnant shortly after borrowing the doll from the sculpture-loan section, hence the demand.[44]

Not only were standing stones visited to promote the fertility of women as described earlier; they were also sometimes visited to promote the growth of the crops, or to encourage rainfall. At Audeby in Lincolnshire, a legend described how Boundell's Stone was beaten with hazel rods to make the rain fall, and how another magic stone was beaten to make the corn grow.[45] Such legends as this may indicate that men were once able to manipulate natural forces to produce the desired effect. Even today, there are reports of people able 'magically' to produce rain where it is needed.[46]

In North Wales, if water was thrown on to the Red Altar, a stone at the end of a stone causeway leading to the lake Llyn Dulyn in Snowdonia, it was said to rain before nightfall.[47] Rain would also fall if a standing stone on the island of Guernsey in the Channel Islands was disturbed. The stone, at La Moye, was locally considered to be a holy stone, and at haymaking time the grass around it was avoided until the rest of the hay was gathered. If this were not done, and the grass cut right up to the stone, it was said that rainstorms would break out.[48]

People would visit the Field of the Bowing near Galtrigal on the Isle of Skye in order to walk three times round and bow to the Bowing Stone. They did this to ensure a good harvest. When a minister came to the area who did not approve of such pagan practices, he had the stone uprooted and thrown into a field. But still people visited the stone, which was then thrown into a ravine by the farmer whose land was being trampled. Eventually the broken pieces were collected and piled up, and the people came to bow to them.[49] Scottish fishermen would bring gifts and baskets of sand to the Kempock Stane, near Gourock, as they believed the stone could affect the weather. They sprinkled sand at the foot of the stone and walked around it, asking for good weather, calm seas and a large catch.[50] A third Scottish site where good weather could be guaranteed if the correct ritual was performed was in Glen Lyon in Tayside. A stone hut called Tigh na Cailliche (the Hag's House) housed three stones: the Bodach (Old Man), the

Cailleach (Hag), and the Nighean (Daughter). During the winter they were left inside the hut, which was kept in good repair by a local shepherd, and in spring the stones were brought outside. They were said to guarantee good pastures and fine weather for the year, and the choice of names suggests a relic of earth goddess worship.[51]

Mircea Eliade describes how many peoples around the world regard standing stones as petrified ancestors, able to produce rain or promote fertility.[52] From the evidence in British folklore, it does not necessarily seem that ancestors as such were being invoked. The Scottish custom just described indicates worship of the earth goddess, or Earth Mother, and the following customs could be interpreted in the same way. They describe how offerings were made to standing stones, usually flowers or food, or even sacrifices. One such custom which survived at least to the end of the eighteenth century was described in his diary by William Fleming, a country gentleman from Furness in what is now south Cumbria but used to be Lancashire.

Friday, May 24, 1801. About 100 yards to the West of Urswick Church in Furness in a Field called Kirkflat, adjoining to the Highway, stands a rough piece of unhewn Limestone, which the Inhabitants of Urswick were accustomed to dress as a Figure of Priapus on Midsummer Day, besmearing it with Sheep Salve, Tar or Butter and covering it with Rags of various Dyes, the Head ornamented with Flowers.

Note the use of the name 'Priapus', who was a Greek god of the male procreative power, and of gardens and vineyards. This use suggests that the custom had some fertility significance.[53]

Flowers and other offerings were made until recently to La Gran'mère du Chimquière, a granite standing stone shaped as a female figure 5 feet 6 inches tall which stands at the gateway to the church of St Martin on Guernsey. Fruit and flowers were placed at her feet, in the hope of good fortune and fertility, and historian J. Stevens Cox spoke to old local inhabitants who could remember placing flowers on La Gran'mère's head or at her feet on May Day, for good luck.[54] Flower garlands were also placed around the largest stone in the circle at Grange by Lough Gur in County Limerick,[55] while in parts of Somerset it was customary on Midsummer Eve to 'Find the biggest stone in the farm and put a bunch of flowers on it for luck' (Taunton Deane, 1920), or 'Climb a hill, make a pile of stones on top and put a bunch of flowers on it for luck' (Quantock Hills).[56] Notice that prehistoric standing stones were not involved in these customs,

La Gran'mère du Chimquière still guards the gateway to St Martin church.

but the principle, of making an offering to a stone (representing the Earth Mother), is the same. In County Armagh, the farm gateposts were sometimes called the man and wife of the house, and the old people put the first two plates of champ (a dish of mashed potatoes made at Hallowe'en) on top of them.[57]

In Cornwall, earth was thrown on Respryn Cross at St Winnow, as witnessed by T. Quiller-Couch in the mid-nineteenth century,[58] while in Scotland it was often customary to pour milk into cups and hollows in stones, to keep the brownies and other supernatural beings happy.[59] Widespread stone worship in Scotland is indicated by the names which some stones still bear, like *clach aoraidh* (worship stone) or *clach sleuchda* (bowing stone), though no details of the customs survive.[60] However, on Orkney, until the destruction of the Stone of Odin in

Arthur's Quoit or Arthur's Stone or Maen Ceti (Stone of Ceti). According to folklore, the capstone was a pebble thrown here by King Arthur who found it in his shoe. The stone is also said to go down to the sea to bathe or drink at certain times, especially Midsummer Eve and All Hallows Eve. These are very special dates, as later chapters will show, and this folklore memory, added to the young girls' custom, suggests that in the past this site was a centre for fertility rituals.

1814, 'it was customary to leave some offering on visiting the stone such as a piece of bread or cheese or rag or even a stone.'[61] In Wales, young girls wishing to see if their lovers were faithful would visit Coetan Arthur (Arthur's Quoit) on the Gower peninsula in West Glamorgan at midnight and full moon, leaving offerings of barley cakes and crawling several times around the stones.[62]

A sacrifice in the form of a ram used to be made at a granite standing stone at Holne in Devon. On the morning of May Day the unfortunate beast was tied to the stone and its throat was cut. After being roasted, the meat was enjoyed as part of a general celebration with dancing, games and wrestling. The meat brought good luck, and those present scrambled for it. A ram-roasting feast was also formerly held near an old stone in a field at Buckland-in-the-Moor in Devon on Midsummer Day. Today the only Devon ram-roasting feast still held is at Kingsteignton on Whit Monday, but no standing stone is involved and the ram is no longer killed publicly.[63] An old custom from the Channel Islands may be a relic of human sacrifice at a standing stone. Boys would make and dress a grotesque figure known as the Bout de l'An (Old Year's End) and after parading it through the streets in a mock funeral procession it would be burnt at the foot of La Longe Rocque or La Palette ès Faïes (The Fairies' Battledore), a standing stone at St-Peter-in-the-Wood on Guernsey.[64]

Although these customary offerings to stones were not apparently made for any particular reason, except perhaps for 'good luck', the evidence in the fertility customs described earlier in the chapter suggests that the offerings were made to stone symbols of the Earth Mother with the intention of placating her, so that she would provide fine weather or rain (when needed), a good harvest, and plenty of children.

4 The shapes of standing stones

'the Spirit of Life dwelt permanently it seemed in these rigid rocks ...'

Michael Harrison, *The Roots of Witchcraft*[1]

As we have just seen, some standing stones symbolized the Earth Mother and her powers; but other stones seem to have individually symbolized the male or female principles. This is indicated in three ways: by their names, by their shapes, and by their arrangement. There are many examples of standing stones with male or female names. In Cornwall there is the stone circle the Merry Maidens with, close by, the Pipers, two tall standing stones. In this case, while the Pipers symbolize the male principle by their phallic shape and their masculine aura, it is the complete circle, not the individual stones in it, which symbolizes the female principle. (Some circles have actually been found to be egg-shaped,[2] but it is not known if this was intended as fertility symbolism.)

The juxtapositioning of male and female stones or groups of stones frequently occurs, and again in Cornwall there is the Men-an-Tol, a good example of this. Two phallic stones stand either side of a roughly circular holed stone, the central hole being large enough for a person to crawl through. Traditionally, people resorted to the Men-an-Tol when they wished to cure certain ailments, and the main feature of the ritual was either to crawl through the hole, or, if the patient was a child, to pass the infant through the hole. This procedure obviously symbolizes birth, the sick person hopefully being reborn to a new life without the unwanted affliction.[3] Whether the holed stone was originally made with such a ritual in mind is of course not known. Archaeologists feel that the three stones which now form the Men-an-Tol may be all that remains of a burial chamber, the holed stone having given access to an otherwise sealed tomb similar to the stone blocking Trethevy Quoit and illustrated in Chapter 3. If the tomb symbolized the womb, as suggested in Chapter 1, then the idea of rebirth through a hole leading into or from that womb follows naturally.

Apart from the holed stone, there is another shape thought to have

The Merry Maidens stone circle and one of the Pipers, near Lamorna in Cornwall.

The Men-an-Tol, near Madron, Cornwall (top). The stones were 're-arranged' in the nineteenth century. Before that they stood in a triangle. A diamond-shaped stone in one of the three stone circles known as the Hurlers (bottom).

symbolized the female principle, a broad diamond. The best-known location of such stones is at Avebury in Wiltshire, where the Kennet Avenue is formed by sarsen standing stones, tall phallic shapes alternating with broad diamond shapes, and each facing its opposite across the avenue. Diamond-shaped stones are also found elsewhere, as for example the impressive stone we saw in one of the Hurlers stone circles on Bodmin Moor in Cornwall (illustrated p. 51). Alexander Keiller, the archaeologist who excavated at Avebury in the 1930s and was instrumental in re-erecting the buried stones, felt that the two shapes symbolized the male and female sexual organs, and further suggested that this indicated that a fertility cult was based at Avebury.[4] The layout of the avenues and henge at Avebury was somewhat serpentine in appearance, and this too may have a bearing on the site's use, the serpent being 'the symbol of immortality and rejuvenescence',[5] and its link with sexuality is graphically shown by the Maryport Serpent Stone, illustrated later in this chapter.

From Avebury we move naturally to Stonehenge, where phallic stones again appear, but there is yet a third way of representing the female principle (if in fact we are not seeing male and female symbolism where it was never intended, always a danger when one begins to look around for a specific feature). At Stonehenge, as the accompanying photograph shows, the phallic bluestones stand surrounded by the female trilithons, two upright stones capped by a third to form a classic female receptive symbol. The layout of the stones at Stonehenge also lends itself to a sexual interpretation. Although the decay of the centuries has resulted in fallen stones and an opening-out of the monument, when it was complete the circles of trilithons and inner bluestones would have given an enclosed feeling to the interior of the site, and it has been suggested that this symbolized the womb. Its opening pointed towards the phallic Heel Stone, and at midsummer the life-giving sun would penetrate into the sacred enclosure, symbolizing the eternal circle of life.

As just mentioned, when looking for male and female stones one begins to see them everywhere, especially phallic stones. Most standing stones are tall, narrow pillars, but that does not necessarily mean that they were intended as phallic symbols. However, when a standing stone has been deliberately shaped so that it is topped by a knob strongly resembling the glans of the penis, then there is little doubt what was intended by the erector. Being so explicit, stones like these have suffered at the hands of prudes and few such stones now

Male and female symbols at Stonehenge?

The phallic stone at Aghowle.

remain, in the British Isles at least. One can be seen in the graveyard of the Romanesque church at Aghowle in County Wicklow, Ireland, a country where many little-known treasures have survived in a wild landscape largely untouched by the twentieth century. Not so lucky was the phallus of St Olan's church in Aghabulloghe, County Cork. The glans of this now 5-foot phallus was destroyed in the last century by a clergyman who did not approve of its being used by the villagers for the cure of illnesses and to bring about successful childbirth.[6]

Similar to the Aghowle phallus is the granite stone at Tømmerby in northern Jutland, Denmark. This phallic stone is 4 feet 3 inches tall, and until 1934 stood outside by the church wall. It is now in the shelter of the church porch. There are spirals and a cross decorating the shaft, and the stone dates from the twelfth century.[7] Overtly phallic stones from many periods are found all over the world, those in southern Ethiopia, usually 6–10 feet tall, being particularly impressive,[8] but since a superfluity of data means that we must confine our survey to the British Isles, we will only very briefly mention two other interesting examples from elsewhere – the fourth-fifth century Pfalzfeld (Hunsrück) stone and the Jacobsthal (Koblenz) stone of similar date, both in Germany. The Pfalzfeld stone originally stood over 6 feet tall, until the male head which capped it was destroyed in the seventeenth century. The Jacobsthal stone stands in the church,

Phallic stones near Soddu in Wolāmo, Southern Ethiopia.

and was resorted to by those wishing for children.[9] Phallic stones have been found in the United States of America by Barry Fell, together with 'Ogam' inscriptions and other engravings relating to fertility rites,[10] but the so-called phallic stones do not have any apparent qualities that make them phallic rather than ordinary standing stones, and the marks on them are more likely to be natural than intentionally carved, according to independent experts who have examined Fell's evidence.[11]

A stone's phallicism is not only shown by its being a clear depiction of the phallus. Some, like the Turoe Stone in County Galway, Ireland, have less visual resemblance to a phallus, but are carved with spiral patterns which according to Philip Rawson 'symbolize what can be translated as the uncanny, numinous power of the transcendent realm, a power identified at bottom with the sexual energy of the earth'.[12] The Turoe Stone, which is 3–4 feet tall, dates from the third or second century BC, and is decorated in a Celtic style known as La Tène. A similar granite stone is at Castlestrange in County Roscommon, which probably dates from the same period as the Turoe Stone and is also decorated in La Tène style. These stones may have been involved in the inauguration ceremonies of kings, and thus embodied the fertility and prosperity of the race.

A stone's location may also indicate its phallic intention. If the elaborate tombs built in prehistoric times were indeed intended to symbolize the womb, as suggested in Chapter 1, then any erect standing stone placed inside the burial chamber could have been intended to symbolize fertility and thus reinforce the tomb's role in the cycle of rebirth. Such a stone stands inside the inner chamber of Bryn-Celli-Ddu, a chambered cairn on the island of Anglesey, North Wales.

According to Dr Anne Ross, expert on the Celtic world, the human head was 'the most highly significant sexual symbol of all for the Celts'.[13] Celts were head-hunters and displayed them on stakes, believing them a source of fertility. They also combined the phallus and the head, carving heads on the glans of phallic stones, and so any stones thus decorated must have symbolized a powerful potency. We have already mentioned the Serpent Stone from Maryport in Cumbria, which by its triple symbolism of phallus, serpent and head contains perhaps the most potent imagery we have seen. It dates from the early third century, and was found in the cemetery of the Roman fort of Alauna (Maryport). The Irish examples of Celtic heads on pillars, which are sometimes carved as rudimentary bodies, are not so clearly sexual in intention, as is shown by the so-called Bishop's Stone at Killadeas in County Fermanagh (illustrated p. 59). However, fertility clearly figures in an American Indian dancing ritual which, according to the engraving by de Bry dating from 1590 (see p. 60), took place around a circle of wooden posts, phallic in shape and carved with human heads. The three women at the centre of the circle were the

The Turoe Stone.

The standing stone inside Bryn-Celli-Ddu.

58

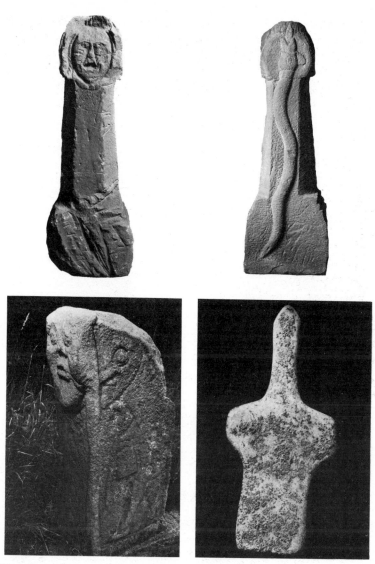

Both faces of the Serpent Stone at Maryport. The stone is 3–4 feet tall (top).

The Bishop's Stone is probably ninth or tenth century. On the west face is a human head and interlaced pattern; on the south face is a bishop or abbot with a crozier and bell (bottom left).

Prehistoric Greek fertility goddess (bottom right).

most beautiful virgins of the tribe, and the rite was obviously intended to promote the fertility of the earth. So again we have a clear link between phallic symbols, human heads, and fertility.

From the standing stone developed the upright Christian cross, which can be seen in a variety of shapes. The cross as we think of it today has arms, and it is interesting to compare such crosses with the prehistoric sculpture from Greece (illustrated p. 59) (its date is *c.* 2500 BC) which depicts a fertility goddess. What we now see as the arms of the cross may originally have been breasts. Some of the older crosses still surviving in Britain are, on the other hand, decidedly phallic in shape. They have no arms, just a tall shaft ending in a knob. This interpretation may be strictly in the eye of the beholder, but we feel that the similarity in shape between the Maen Achwyfan cross illustrated here and the Maryport Serpent Stone illustrated earlier is too close to be simply coincidence.

This is not the only sexual symbolism to be found in Christian architecture, and in the next chapter we shall be looking at explicitly

Virginia Indians engaged in a fertility dance.

sexual carvings actually found on church buildings. But to return to the phallic shape: does the church building itself carry a phallic representation, in the form of the church spire? Some of the oldest spires may strike the unprejudiced viewer as having echoes of phallicism, such as the spire of the Old Priory Church on Caldey Island in Dyfed (illustrated p. 62). To compare a church spire with a phallus is not so far-fetched or irreverent as it might at first seem. We have just described the similarities between Christian crosses and standing stones, and how the one developed from the other. It is likely that the church spire, too, was originally inspired by the standing stone. The spire and the standing stone can both be seen as conveyers of natural energies from sky to earth.

There are a few cases of stones being shaped to represent the whole female body; or sometimes a natural stone has needed no extra shaping for it to be interpreted as a human body. The Blind Fiddler, a standing stone in Cornwall, looks from some angles like a bulky figure; while The White Wife, a 4-foot standing stone at Carnalridge in County

Two old crosses which are phallic in appearance. *Left*, Maen Achwyfan, a tall tenth- or eleventh-century cross standing near Whitford in Clwyd, and *right* St Piran's Cross near the eighth-century St Piran's Oratory on Penhale Sands near Perranporth, Cornwall. The carved figure in the bottom panel on Maen Achwyfan is phallic.

The first monastery on Caldey Island was founded in the fifth century, and the old Priory Church of St Illtud dates from the thirteenth to fourteenth centuries.

The White Wife.

Antrim, seems to have a dual sexuality. A round stone is cemented on top of the tall stone, and from one side the stone looks phallic. From the other, however, it is said to resemble an old woman in a cape. The stone used to be whitewashed every year, but the significance of this act escapes us, unless it was similar to the offerings made to some stones, as described in the previous chapter. A Welsh female stone was also whitewashed. This stone stood, and maybe still stands, in the Lady's Field (Cae'r Ladi) which is near Glasfryn Lake in the parish of Llangybi on the Lleyn Peninsula in Gwynedd. From the nearby house, the stone looked like a woman hurrying along, with her veil and skirt blowing in the wind. Someone who lived nearby remembered the stone actually being dressed in a bonnet and shawl, obviously to reinforce its female characteristics. Not only that, but the field was also haunted by a tall, well-dressed female ghost, who was seen as late as the last century, in the neighbouring house as well as in the field.[14]

In a case such as that of the stone in the Lady's Field, we have no clues as to when the stone was first revered as a female stone, though we can guess it was many hundreds of years ago. The antiquity of stones located in prehistoric tombs is clearly indicated, and in prehistoric tombs in France there have been found several stones carved so as to represent a female figure. Again this could have been so as to reinforce the idea of tomb as womb, and contrasts strongly with our earlier description of a phallic stone inside a Welsh tomb.

Two stones roughly carved to represent the female body can be seen outdoors on Guernsey in the Channel Islands. One, La Gran'mère du Chimquière, was described and illustrated in the previous chapter. On p. 66 we see La Gran'mère du Castel or Câtel, who stands to the north of the west porch in the churchyard of the Câtel church. Her existence was unknown until a hundred years ago. In 1878 she was found buried a foot below the floor at the entrance to the chancel. Her presence there possibly indicates the dedication of the Christian church to the ancient goddess whose sacred site it was usurping. The stone, of local granite, stands 6 feet 6 inches tall.[15]

It seems natural that the men of prehistory should have recognized the phallic qualities of certain stones, and that sometimes they should have sought to enhance those qualities by making the stone more closely resemble the male generative organ. A people to whom the continuance of life and fertility was of perpetual importance would have seen these stones as reinforcing their preoccupation. While they on a small scale perpetuated their own fertility, the Earth Mother on a

A Neolithic 'goddess' from Croizard, Marne.

La Gran'mère du Castel.

much larger scale was encouraged to perpetuate hers. But did the phallic stones 'merely' symbolize the sexual energy of the earth and man? As Michael Harrison comments: 'it was not the phallic shape which first made such objects holy', but the conviction that 'the *permanently* phallic shape – or, rather, the *permanent* rigidity – betokened the permanent residence therein of that magically rigidifying Spirit of Life, which visited men only sporadically, but which honoured these stocks and stones with Its ineffable Presence continuously.'[16] Can we take this a step further and suggest that the stones were not only symbols, but actual tools, carefully placed for very good reasons? They may have actually been huge stone phalluses, capable of accumulating natural energy and directing it into the earth – impregnating and fertilizing the Earth Mother.

5 Church carvings: sexual themes, green men and dragons

'The Earth-Mother embodies the archetype of fecundity, of inexhaustible creativity.'

Mircea Eliade, *Myths, Dreams and Mysteries*[1]

A church might seem a strange place to find a carving of a naked woman displaying her genitals, but there are nearly 40 such carvings in England, Scotland and Wales, and about 75 in Ireland (over 30 of the latter on castles). Carvings depicting phallic and other sexual themes have also been found, but the female carvings are the most frequently seen, and these are known by the strange name of 'Sheela-na-gig'. No one is really sure what this name means. It came from an old man in Ireland who was asked what this type of carving was called, and he may have been saying, in Irish, *'Sighle na gcíoch'* – which possibly meant 'Sheila of the paps', though the breasts are rarely emphasized in these carvings. That may have been simply the local name for one carving.[2] Another interpretation is that 'Sheela' was really 'Sithlach' (Holy Lady), 'na' is 'of the', and 'Gig' was 'gog', a variant of 'god', the whole adding up to 'the holy lady of the god', or 'mother goddess'.[3] Yet another suggestion is that the old man said *'chilo-nagi'* – 'The Idle Hole' – and that he was using an ancient pagan language.[4]

But whatever the old man may really have meant by 'Sheela-na-gig', it is an awkward and meaningless term, now beginning to be replaced by the more explicit 'exhibitionist'. This covers all classes of sexual carving, and indicates their true nature, that they are simply *displaying* their genitals. Such carvings are not erotic, as they are sometimes described. 'Erotic' means 'arousing sexual desire or giving sexual pleasure', which is not in the nature of these often hag-like women. Nor were they intended to be obscene. The concept of obscenity varies from age to age and from culture to culture, and at the time when exhibitionist figures were carved the display of genitals was probably not considered obscene in the way it is today. Later defacement, and probable destruction, of these carvings indicates a change in attitude over the centuries. Some carvings have survived only because of strong local feeling (especially in Ireland), or because they were hidden away in some churches and many people were unaware of their existence, or because they were misinterpreted. The famous Kilpeck carving, the interpretation of which seems obvious to us today, was in 1842 described as a fool – 'the cut in his chest, the way to his heart, denotes it is always open and to all alike'.[5]

It is clear, then, that the artists' intention when carving the female exhibitionist figures was display. But why display female genitals in this way? The question is complex, and is made more complicated by the problem of dating the carvings and tracing their origins.[6] Experts see a close link between many exhibitionists and Romanesque (Norman/French/Spanish, ninth-twelfth centuries) motifs, there being hundreds of such carvings in France and Spain which have received little attention. When a carving has obviously always been

This hag-like figure (left) is one of the best preserved female exhibitionist carvings. It came from a ruined church at Cavan in County Cavan and is now in the National Museum of Ireland in Dublin.
Many of the English female exhibitionists located out of doors are now very worn and almost unrecognizable, but this one at Buckland in Buckinghamshire (right), above the Priest's Door of the parish church, is still clear. Nevertheless the carving was identified to us by a local resident as an effigy of the last man to be hanged on Hangman's Hill!

part of the church fabric, and the construction of that church can be accurately dated, then there is no problem. Kilpeck church, for example, in Hereford and Worcester, is a masterpiece of the local school of Norman sculptors. The south doorway is one of the most elaborately carved in Britain (a 'green man' among the carvings can be seen later in this chapter), and the corbel table which decorates the outside walls contains many strange and well-preserved carvings, including Britain's most notable female exhibitionist. All this work can be fairly accurately dated to *c.* 1140. But in many other instances where the exhibitionist is outside the church it is carved on a piece of stone inserted into the wall, and it is hard to tell exactly when this was done, especially if the church has been altered many times over the centuries. But rather than get embroiled in the intricacies of dating,

South Tawton church in Devon is rich in mediaeval roof bosses, which include carvings of foliate heads, spirals, a possible maze, and this female exhibitionist. Dated to the fourteenth or fifteenth centuries, this boss appears to be in its original position, and if so, it is doubtful if the carving was intended to warn people against sin because it is practically impossible to see it from below without a strong torch. We had great difficulty taking this photograph because the roof was so dark, and the camera had to be focused by guess. We were not able to study the carving properly until the photographs were printed. The figure seems to grow from foliage, which may indicate a fertility significance.

The well-preserved female exhibitionist at Kilpeck in Hereford and Worcester.

we will concern ourselves with the carvings themselves, and what significance they may have had.

Having been exposed to the weather for hundreds of years, those female exhibitionist carvings on the outside of buildings are often well worn, and it is only the keen expert eye that can interpret them. Few are now totally clear, as the illustrations here show, but in the Middle Ages (*c.* 1000 to the fifteenth century) when they were newly carved, their nature was obvious at a glance. The onlooker's attention would be drawn immediately to the woman's genitals, often actively displayed by use of the hands. Why? And why, especially, on churches? Many explanations have been advanced, most of them having some validity, and the answer could combine features from all of them, since such questions are rarely easily answered.

Perhaps the most prosaic explanation is that which places the carvings in a Christian context and classifies them as reminders of, and warnings against, the sins of the flesh. But it has been suggested that such a warning would be counter-productive, as female exhibitionist carvings would *remind* the sensualists of what the Church would rather they forgot![7] Anthony Weir, who has made an intensive study of exhibitionist figures and related carvings, has pointed out to us that 'The sins of Lust and Concupiscence were/are an obsession of Christian culture', and that throughout Europe there are carvings which portray this in graphic terms. In the carving illustrated (p. 74), from the church at Ôo in France, a lascivious woman is tormented by a snake which issues from her vulva and bites her breast. The female exhibitionists we see in Britain were generally carved later than those elsewhere in Europe and do not have the same horrifying impact. They may be a revival of the genre, carved with less skill by amateurs.[8]

All the remaining explanations for the female exhibitionists suggest that the inspiration for these carvings stems from a time before the arrival of Christianity. Celtic scholar Dr Anne Ross suggests that some of the early carvings portray 'the territorial or war-goddess in her hag-like aspect' as described in pagan Celtic tales, and that their intention was both to promote fertility and avert evil.[9] However, nowhere in northern Europe are there *female* exhibitionist images from before the tenth century, whereas the Celts delighted in *male* carvings.[10] Significantly, male or female genital display has, for many centuries, been thought to be a powerful means of repelling evil (and, in India at least, lightning),[11] and this belief may be one reason why such unlikely carvings were incorporated into church buildings. But if

A Post-Romanesque carving from Ôo church in Haute-Garonne, France, and now in the Musée des Augustans, Toulouse.

the carvings depicted a pagan goddess, or even the Earth Mother herself, as has been widely suggested,[12] surely the Church authorities would have been loth to display them? Perhaps, though, they felt that Christianity had overcome the power of pagan goddesses, and saw the carvings simply as anti-evil symbols. Or possibly the Churchman in those centuries, especially in the more remote areas, combined the ancient pagan practices with the newer Christian ones. There is a little evidence that this was so. In 1282, the priest at Inverkeithing in Fife had to appear before his bishop for leading a fertility dance at Easter round a phallic figure,[13] and in the fourteenth century the Bishop of Exeter was shocked to learn that the monks of Frithelstock Priory in Devon were wont to worship a statue like 'the unchaste Diana' at an altar in the woods.[14] These two recorded incidents of continuing paganism spanning the 1200s and 1300s, and from opposite ends of Britain, suggest a multitude of pagan survivals of which no trace remains. The discovery by Professor Geoffrey Webb of phallic symbols concealed inside the altars of a number of pre-1348 (the year the Black Death spread to Europe) churches[15] supports the view that paganism was not immediately suppressed by Christianity, a belief which is further supported by the many church carvings with pagan overtones, not just the exhibitionists with which this chapter deals, but also the foliate heads or 'green men' to be described later in this chapter, and other grotesques. Elsewhere in Europe, phalli were widely worshipped in Christian churches, in some places until the eighteenth century, or maybe even later.[16]

But it is hardly surprising that there should be evidence of the continued practice of pagan rites, since it is widely recognized that the original simple message of Christ has been incorporated into a large traditional body of dogma and practice, gathered from widely diverse sources. This has evolved into the variety of Christian sects which exist today. Brian Branston links the old and new religions in his *The Lost Gods of England*:

... the death and resurrection of Jesus was a necessity that the world might live. This was what the 'new' story, the 'new' myth, the 'new' religion meant to the ordinary people, and it was compatible with many fertility rites and observances such as the blessing of the plough, of rivers and the sea, with conjuration of fruit trees, with prayers for good seasons, rain and the general fertility of the earth, with thanksgiving at harvest, with mourning and rejoicing at Easter for the death of the god and his resurrection.[17]

Some of the symbolism absorbed by the Christian religion, when

This female exhibitionist does not indicate her genitals with her hands and is thought to be a late carving, perhaps seventeenth century. It was set up by a holy well at Castlemagner in County Cork, and there are clear signs of rubbing on the hands, forehead, stomach and thighs. Pilgrims would make the sign of the cross on the carving as part of the ritual at the well.

studied closely, appears to have direct links with fertility. For example, the almond-shaped mandorla or vesica piscis which surrounds holy figures in religious paintings in one sense symbolizes the vulva.[18] In an earlier chapter we saw how the cross could have been derived from the female figure. It has also been seen as a phallic symbol, in its simplest form as the penis and testicles,[19] and therefore could combine both male and female symbolism.

There is also some evidence that the female exhibitionists had a fertility significance, though this may only be a late development. Interpreted as symbols of the Earth Mother, these powerful carvings depicting her in her procreative role must have impressed people with the belief that her power could be transferred to them. Of these carvings E. M. Guest wrote in 1935: 'Some of these stones are still touched to facilitate childbirth.'[20] Referring to Palaeolithic cultures, E. O. James remarked that 'any object directly associated with the female principle and generative functions seems to have been regarded as a symbol of vitality capable of transferring its fertilizing

Male genitals decorated the top of a window at Smithstown Castle in County Clare.

properties from one person or one thing to another.'[21] He was thinking of the 'Venus figurines' which we described and illustrated in Chapter 2, and it is interesting to consider whether the mediaeval female exhibitionist carvings are in fact descended from those figures of around 25,000 years ago.

So far we have described only female exhibitionists. Male exhibitionist carvings have also been found, but these have received less attention than the female carvings. The name invented for them, 'Seamus na mogairle',[22] is as awkward as 'Sheela-na-gig', and is probably best ignored in favour of 'male exhibitionist'. Some examples are illustrated here, and it can be seen that the carvings vary from isolated male genitals to men with erect phalli. In the Whittlesford, Cambridgeshire, carving, a female exhibitionist is accompanied by a male exhibitionist who has animal characteristics. As with the female carvings, the interpretation of the male exhibitionists is uncertain, but some, particularly those showing the phallus alone, may have been intended to avert evil. The Romans used

His pigeon-toed stance forms a frame for the genital display of this male exhibitionist at Ballycloghduff in County Westmeath (left).
The exact origin of this carving (right), now in the Margam Stones Museum in West Glamorgan, is not known, but it is probably local, and possibly from the ruined abbey.

The carving on an exterior wall at Whittlesford church (top).
A phallus carved on a paving stone in the courtyard of the headquarters
building at Chesters Roman fort in Northumberland (bottom).

the phallus as a good luck sign and it is found quite often at Roman sites. There are good examples at Chesters (Cilurnum) Roman fort on Hadrian's Wall and at Maryport (Alauna) Roman fort in Cumbria, both illustrated here. The symbol retained its potency down the ages, as shown by the two phalli found as part of larger carvings in a Welsh farmhouse. Dated to the late seventeenth century, these carvings are thought to have originally flanked the entrance to Kennixton farmhouse. (In 1951 the farmhouse was dismantled and taken from its original site at Llangennydd in the Gower peninsula of South Wales and re-erected at the Welsh Folk Museum.) The oak carvings are about 16 inches tall, and show legless men above prominent erect phalli. Dr Anne Ross commented that 'the emblems above the figures also strike one as having a certain phallic appearance.' Other pairs of phallic or hermaphrodite figures have been found flanking house entrances, and it is generally assumed that they were placed there to protect the building and its occupants against evil spirits and witches.[23] Perhaps this was originally the significance of a figure called Jack Stag which once stood on top of the market cross at Glastonbury

Penis and vulva carved on a stone from Maryport Roman fort.

The carving from Kennixton farmhouse.

Two 'tongue-pokers': (top) on the rood-screen in Finchingfield church, Essex; (bottom) a roof boss in Withersfield church, Suffolk.

in Somerset. Removed in 1808, it is now in the local museum, but it is so worn that no one is quite sure whether 'Jack' is male or female, though the name suggests the former.[24]

Also thought to be phallic in intent are the numerous church carvings depicting grotesque faces with protruding tongues. Although Lady Raglan, who wrote on 'green man' carvings, felt that the protruding tongue signified death by hanging, Mrs M. D. Anderson was one of the first writers on church symbolism to identify 'tongue-pokers' as fertility symbols. She referred to a particular carving in support of this idea. It is on the fourteenth-century rood screen in Willingham church, Cambridgeshire, and shows a figure which 'has a leg extended along either side of the corner; the hands hold the mouth open, and a protruding tongue of exaggerated size covers the genital region'. She also noted that the 'rude' habit of sticking out one's tongue may be linked to the 'tongue as phallus' symbolism.[25] Again the intention behind such carvings may have been protection against evil. Another style of carving with sexual overtones is the 'mouth-

A worn 'mouth-puller' carving on the exterior wall of Torksey church in Lincolnshire.

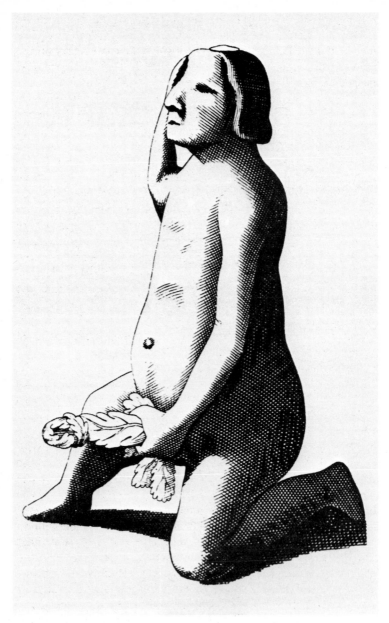

Jack of Hilton.

84

puller', where a grotesque figure uses its hands to pull open its mouth – a gesture which closely parallels the female exhibitionist pulling open her vulva. The Willingham carving noted by Mrs Anderson also includes this action, and so the carving is in fact hermaphrodite, incorporating both male and female sexual symbolism.

There is a wide variety of ways in which mediaeval church carvers illustrated sexual themes, such as carvings of women suckling serpents, groin-biting beasts, foot-suckers and foot-swallowers, and couples copulating, but most of these seem to be some way removed from the direct message of the female exhibitionists, and unlikely to have any relationship to the main theme of this book, fertility.[26] We end this discussion of sexual carvings with a few oddities which do have a fertility significance, and although not carvings, they do reiterate our earlier statement, that attitudes towards obscenity have changed. The unusual brass figure illustrated here by an engraving was known as Jack of Hilton, and was believed to be of Etruscan origin. It was used in an annual ceremony on New Year's Day, when water was poured into it and after heating on a fire, the steam would 'blow the fire' while a goose was driven round the fire several times before being taken away and cooked for the Lord of Hilton. This ceremony took place at Hilton Hall, Essington in Staffordshire, until the early seventeenth century.[27]

Personal fertility was ensured, or so the believer hoped, by the wearing of a phallic amulet. These were once common all over Europe, and in India, China and Japan. At various times all manner of personal items have taken sexual forms, such as walking sticks, snuff boxes, matchboxes, and doorstops. In Victorian times, even, there were cast-iron doorstops in the shape of bare-breasted female figures lying with legs apart. And the humble horseshoe, still fastened over the house door as a symbol of good luck, may once have been seen as a symbol of the female genitals, and the 'good luck' may originally have been fertility.[28] This is similar to the Roman usage of the phallus as a good luck symbol, and their inclusion of phallic carvings on their buildings.

Pagan themes are often to be found in church carvings, sometimes blatantly and sometimes subtly portrayed. One character who can often be seen is the 'green man' (or preferably 'foliate head', a strictly factual term which avoids a possibly mistaken identification of a complex symbol). Kathleen Basford, who has written a book on the subject,[29] has traced the foliate head back to Roman art of the first century AD, and has located many examples of this type of carving in

The link between the horseshoe and fertility is shown in this old photograph of a wedding being performed over the anvil at the Blacksmith's Shop in Gretna Green. However, we wonder if this marriage lasted: the horseshoe is unfortunately inverted and thus its power and luck have drained away.

Europe. The theme spread to Britain soon after the Norman Conquest, but the majority of carvings seem to date from the thirteenth, fourteenth and fifteenth centuries. Foliage and heads (usually human, sometimes animal) are the main features, but there are variations in design.

1. A human face peeps out through foliage.

2. A human face is formed of foliage, usually shown by the hair and edges of the face being carved as foliage.

3. A face sprouts foliage from the mouth (most often), or sometimes from the nose, eyes, or ears.

Foliate heads may be found carved on roof bosses, corbels, capitals, fonts, tympana, tombs (these all stone), screens, bench-ends and misericords (these all wood), in fact wherever there are carvings in churches. It is so widespread a theme that no complete list of British carvings has been, or could be, compiled. They are likely to be seen in any church with pre-1500 features, and several of those we have photographed were discovered unexpectedly.

Among the rich carving around the doorway at Kilpeck church, Hereford and Worcester, is a grotesque head with foliage springing from its mouth.

87

What did the mediaeval craftsmen intend when they carved these figures? Were they purely decorative, copied from foreign models and bearing no message? Some may well have been. The carvings vary so much, as do the twentieth-century interpretations of them, that it is clear that there was never an all-embracing motivation behind the foliate heads. Bearing that in mind, let us consider the ideas that have been suggested. Most popular is the 'Green Man' interpretation, that the carvings represented the 'Jack in the Green' figure of the May celebrations. The similarity between the foliage framework hiding a man who peeped out through a small hole, and the carved face peering out through leaves, was first noticed by Lady Raglan, who also seems to have been the first person to identify the foliate head theme in church carving.[30] Since the Jack in the Green (whom we shall describe more fully in Chapter 10) seems to have symbolized the renewal of life in spring, the link with the church carving is compelling, especially with the most often seen variation, the face with foliage sprouting from it. Variants of this theme suggest that the carvings depict tree-spirits or demons (the faces are often ugly or evil), or illustrate the

This powerful fifteenth-century foliate head carved on a roof boss dominates the chancel of Sampford Courtenay church in Devon.

continuance of tree-worship, a practice which will be described in the next chapter. Followers of the 'Old Religion', or witchcraft, have seen the foliate head as the 'Old God',[31] but just as plausible (or implausible, depending on one's beliefs) is the idea that these heads, and the other heads without foliage that are seen so often in churches, represent a survival of the head-cult which was so widespread and

A foliate head in the chancel of Old Radnor church, Powys.

important in the Celtic culture. In support of the idea that the carvings represent gods of some kind, it is interesting to note that there are carvings of Roman deities emerging from leaves; for example on the capital of the third-century AD Jupiter column from Corinium (Cirencester) in Gloucestershire, which depicts two male and two female deities.[32]

Kathleen Basford feels that the 'Jack in the Green' or 'May King' explanation so widely accepted is unlikely to explain many foliate head carvings, because so many of the faces are unattractive: 'some of the Green Men look crosseyed and crapulous and others might well be suffering from a hang-over'.[33] The carvings illustrated in this chapter have a variety of expressions, which tends to support her sentiment. Some, she feels, 'probably represent lost souls or sinners', with the source of the leaves indicating that sins were committed by the organ thus indicated.[34] But some of the carvings have neutral expressions, for example the simple but striking bench-end in Bishops Lydeard church, Somerset, which depicts a face both naïve and beneficent. Carvings such as this suggest strongly to us that the vital force responsible for the continuance of all life was being depicted. As part of this symbolism is the implicit statement, acceptable to Christian and pagan alike, that at death man's body returns (or should return, if the natural cycle is followed) to earth, and from its decay springs new life. Man and tree are inextricably linked in a natural cycle of death and rebirth, and this, we feel, is the inspiration behind at least some carvings of foliate heads.[35] To look at them is to be reminded of the earth's never-failing energy which year after year ensures that life continues to flourish.

This theme of the earth spirit and the fruitfulness which results from it is also depicted in church carvings, but often they are hidden away. An ornately carved wooden screen may bear much intricate leaf carving, unexpectedly incorporating a dragon from whose mouth emerges foliage and fruit. This may only be noticed if the whole screen is closely examined, and its concealment suggests a sign placed there for the initiate. In Christian iconography, 'The dragon is equated with the serpent, "that old serpent", the power of evil, the Devil, the Tempter, the enemy of God; it also represents death and darkness, paganism and heresy.'[36] But in China 'the dragon and the serpent, invested with the most profound and all-embracing cosmic significance, are symbols for "rhythmic life".'[37] Bunches of grapes, a potent fertility symbol, are often part of these dragon carvings, and to

The Bishops Lydeard carving dates from the early sixteenth century.

us these symbols express the idea that whatever the dominant creed and dogma, the fertility and renewal of man and earth are inextricably linked, and this knowledge will be at the root of any effective religious practice. So the appearance of these carvings in Christian churches need not be considered incongruous.

This fruitful dragon in Sampford Courtenay church, Devon, sprouts foliage and fruit from its mouth and tail.

6 Holy wells and sacred trees

'... in fairy tales a well is often the gate to the underworld and specifically to
the domain of the earth mother ... the tree is ... the earth phallus, the male
principle jutting out of the earth ...'

Erich Neumann, *The Great Mother*[1]

Natural water supplies in the form of rivers, streams, pools, springs
and wells have seemingly always been venerated, which is not
surprising in view of the vital role water plays in man's existence. By
the time the Celtic culture was established in Britain, which happened
several hundred years BC,[2] water worship was an important and
complex aspect of religious practice. Bronze Age people and the early
Celts saw wells as entrances to the underworld and cut ritual wells,
pits and shafts deep into the earth. One near Stonehenge in Wiltshire
is about 110 feet deep, ending in a well. Objects presumably intended
as offerings to the gods – pottery, bones, coins, pebbles – were thrown
into these shafts.[3] Such archaeological evidence for early well worship
is later supplemented by literary evidence in Celtic times, and the
evidence shows that the water cult was widespread throughout
Europe. The Celts believed that water conveyed fertility, and the
Celtic mother goddesses, also much involved with fertility as we saw
in Chapters 1 and 2, became linked to sacred water sources. One well
which illustrates the cult was discovered in 1876 at the Roman fort of
Brocolitia (Carrawburgh) on Hadrian's Wall. The well was dedicated to
Coventina, who was probably a local goddess adopted by the Romans.
Over 14,000 coins, together with other offerings like glass, pottery,
and bronze figures, dating from pre-Roman times up to the fourth
century AD, were found in the well, as were twenty-four altars,
possibly hidden there when the shrine was attacked. A well-preserved
stone tablet shows Coventina lying on water plants and an urn, and
holding another plant.[4] The well is still visible, but because of marshy
ground is unapproachable except in very dry weather.

The Celtic cult of the head was also associated with water worship.
There is varied evidence for this, such as the discovery of human skulls
in wells and pools (including one in Coventina's Well), and traditional
tales in which people are decapitated and their heads thrown into
wells.[5] Some wells miraculously appeared where a severed head fell,

A Roman title from Caerleon (Roman Isca) in Gwent, showing a Celtic goddess rising from a fountain (top left).

The stone tablet depicting Coventina is now in the Museum of Antiquities in Newcastle upon Tyne (top right).

A 'Christianized' fresh-water spring at Fulking in West Sussex (bottom).

such as St Winifred's Well at Holywell in Clwyd. Prince Caradoc had evil intentions towards the virgin St Winifred, to which she did not respond, and so he beheaded her. Where her head fell, water gushed from the earth; and Winifred was miraculously restored to life by St Beuno.[6] The well became famous and is one of the few holy wells in Britain still much visited. Also in Wales, it was long the custom at certain wells to drink the water out of a human skull, and this custom survived into the present century at one Pembrokeshire well.[7] To the Celts the severed head had strong fertility associations, as we have already shown in Chapter 4 where heads on phallic stones are described and illustrated.

Even when Christianity ostensibly ousted the pagan cults in Britain, water worship survived. The sacred wells became 'holy' wells, and the goddesses who had presided over them became nymphs and guardians of wells, or saints to whom the wells were dedicated. The ghosts of white ladies traditionally associated with some wells and pools may also be dim memories of pagan goddesses. So although there were superficial changes, well worship continued as strongly as ever. People visited the holy wells to seek cures for a variety of illnesses, often leaving offerings in the water (just as people today still drop coins into so-called wishing wells), and most wells were famed for their ability to cure, some curing only specific diseases, others curing many different ailments. Some wells were claimed to have the power of divination or prophecy, and some were visited on a certain day in the year, the people taking sugar and liquorice and mixing it with the water before drinking it. Such practices are now rare, but in Wychwood Forest (Oxfordshire) the Lady's Well at Wilcote is still visited on Palm Sunday by children who take liquorice to mix with the water.[8]

Well worship has also survived into the twentieth century in the form of well-dressing, which was once done in many parts of Britain but now survives only in Derbyshire and Staffordshire. The dressing was done with flowers and greenery, one example from many in the past being the 'Halliwell (Holy Well) Wakes' at Rorrington, a hamlet near Chirbury on the Shropshire/Wales border. On Ascension Day the local people would meet at the holy well on the hillside at Rorrington Green. The well had been decorated with 'a bower of green boughs, rushes, and flowers' and a maypole was erected. The people 'used to walk round the hill with fife, drum, and fiddle, dancing and frolicking as they went', and this was followed by feasting, dancing and drinking. They drank the well water – and also ale which was specially brewed for the occasion. They threw pins into the well, and they ate special flat spiced buns marked with a cross. To keep one would bring good luck, it was said. When the man who brewed the ale died in the early 1830s, the wake was no longer held.[9]

The well-dressing ceremonies which have survived in the north Midlands involve much skill and hard work. Originally the wells were decorated with wreaths and garlands, but about 1818 the style of decoration we see today was introduced. Elaborate pictures illustrating Christian themes are carefully constructed from natural objects like flowers, petals, leaves, grasses, cones, seeds, berries, beans, rice and pebbles, all pressed into moist clay on a wooden screen. The pictures are then displayed at the wells for a few days, and thanksgiving services are held. The best-known well-dressing celebration is at Tissington in Derbyshire, where five wells are dressed on Ascension Day. Others in the county are dressed at different times in the summer – at Buxton, Barlow, Wirksworth, Youlgreave, Stoney Middleton, Eyam, Hope and Tideswell.[10] The well-dressing ceremonies have now been adopted by the Christian Church and are today performed as a thanksgiving for water. The veneration of the spirit or goddess of the water has long been forgotten.

There were once literally thousands of holy wells in Britain and Ireland (Francis Jones studied nearly 1,200 in his *The Holy Wells of Wales*), but many are now sadly lost – abandoned and overgrown. Some, like the one at Holywell described earlier, are still active, but now possess a very strong aura of emotional Christianity. Others have survived against all odds, hidden away in the depths of the countryside and still able to evoke feelings of veneration for the Earth Mother, as here symbolized by a mysterious pool of life-giving water. When we have visited such places, it has not been difficult to understand how our ancestors came to venerate the water goddesses and to call upon them for aid in matters of fertility. The people living near Gellionen Well, which was near Pontardawe in West Glamorgan, used to perform a ritual at the well when they needed rain. According to a man who as a child in the early nineteenth century had seen the ritual performed, they would dance on a green spot near the well and throw flowers and herbs at each other. They would also sing old ballads and play 'kiss-in-the-ring' (was this all that remained of a fertility ritual?). The leader went to the well and three times cried 'Bring us rain!' The assembled company then filled bowls with well water and threw it

Reading psalms at the Coffin Well, Tissington, during the well-dressing ceremonies (top).

A Christian chapel has been built over the holy well at Holywell in Clwyd, and a large bathing pool accommodates the still numerous pilgrims (bottom left). By contrast, the Red Well is hidden in a wood near Knapwell in Cambridgeshire and is very difficult to find (bottom right).

about, or took it home and scattered it on the garden. It was said that rain always followed this ritual.[11]

Although such agricultural links with holy wells are rare, the traditional story of how St Milburga's Well at Stoke St Milborough in Shropshire came into being also contains a hint of agricultural fertility lore. St Milburga was fleeing from her enemies on horseback, and after two days and nights of hard riding she reached the village. She fell from her horse in a faint and struck her head on a stone. Some men sowing barley nearby ran to help her, but there was no water to hand. St Milburga told her horse to strike the rock with his hoof, and when he did so a spring of water gushed forth. She commanded 'Holy water, henceforth and for ever flow freely', and turning to the newly sown barley she also commanded it to grow. Instantly green blades appeared. She instructed the men to tell her pursuers that she had passed by when they were sowing their barley. And so that same evening, when they were reaping the barley which had grown apace during the day, the men were able to baffle St Milburga's pursuers with their honest but misleading information.[12]

Although many people visited holy wells seeking cures for ailments, women often resorted to them specifically to cure their barrenness. The traditional pagan worship of mother goddesses at holy wells, the natural interpretation of the well as a secret entrance into the body of the Earth Mother or even as her womb, the belief in the life-giving or procreative powers of water – all combined to instil in people the certainty that the holy well was the source of fertility. Even without the folklore traditions which follow, there is evidence of the fertility beliefs in the finding of pins in very many holy wells. They were one of the votive objects regularly thrown into the wells, and as Anne Ross comments, pins were 'invariably associated with childbirth'.[13] We begin our survey of the fertility folklore of holy wells on the distant Aran Islands off the west coast of Ireland, where women prayed for children at St Eaney's Well, while men visited another well not far away for the same purpose.[14] On the island of Skye, off the west coast of Scotland, there were several fertility wells, one near Elgol by Loch Scavaig and another at Strolamas which would even produce twins if correctly used. The Tobar an Torraidh or Well of Fertility, a third fertility well on Skye, was reputed to make barren cattle fertile, and was also secretly visited by barren women.[15] Also in Scotland, there was a well used to cure barrenness in Perthshire, at St Fillans at the eastern end of Loch Earn,[16] another known as St Columba's Font in the old churchyard of Killianan by Loch Ness,[17] while the Bride's Well near Corgarff in Grampian was visited by the bride on the evening before her marriage. She would bathe her feet and upper body in well water, to ensure that she would have children, and she placed a little bread and cheese in the well so that they would never go hungry.[18]

In the late 1860s, two men were by chance able secretly to watch a fertility ritual being practised at a holy well, the well of Melshach in the parish of Kennethmont in Grampian, and this account of the event is by J. M. McPherson.

On the first Sunday of May, a keeper, accompanied by an expert from Aberdeen, set out for the moors to investigate grouse disease then prevalent. From a distance, they spied a group of women round the well. With the aid of a field-glass, the men watched their movements. The women, with garments fastened right up under their arms and with hands joined, were dancing in a circle round the well. An aged crone sat in their midst, and dipping a small vessel in the water, kept sprinkling them. They were married women who had proved childless and had come to the well to experience its fertilizing virtues. No doubt words had been repeated, but the two observers were too far off to hear. There are many marks here of a primitive rite. The Convention took place on the first Sunday of May. The women were formed in a circle with their skirts kilted up, and the old woman, the presiding priestess of the well, administered its waters by sprinkling. Sprinkling was one of the methods employed at the ancient fertility wells.[And see Chapter 11, where other water sprinkling customs are described.] But so little is known of the ritual at these wells when the object was to cure sterility, that the account of this ceremonial at Melshach receives an added importance. The remarkable thing is that the custom lingered so late.[19]

Several Welsh holy wells were also known for their power to bestow fertility, for example St Winifred's Well at Holywell (Clwyd) and Ffynnon y Filiast and Ffynnon y Brenin, both in Llaniestyn parish in Gwynedd.[20] In England the most northerly of several fertility wells we have on record is the Bore Well near Bingfield in Northumberland. On the Sunday following Old Midsummer Day (4 July), a fair was held there. Female pilgrims wishing for children would pray at the well, and the annual fair was still being held in 1878.[21] In Cambridgeshire there was a fertility well at Burwell which would ensure male twins for women who drank the water,[22] while at Oxford Child's Well 'had vertue to make women that were barren to bring forth children'.[23] In Somerset the St Agnes Well at Whitestaunton is said to have been visited by Queen Henrietta, wife of King Charles I, and that she wished for a child there, with a successful outcome.[24] The

Pipe Well at Liskeard in Cornwall ensured fertility to couples standing on a certain stone to drink the water,[25] and there was also a fertility well at Looe in Cornwall. In the same county the water of a well in Sithney parish, near Helston, made women barren! There seems to have been as great a demand for water from this well as for water from fertility wells, in those pre-contraceptive days, and women came from miles around. The parson did not approve, and the well was filled in.[26]

Observance of traditional rituals was particularly strong in Ireland, as is shown by this description of local practices in connection with holy wells.

Dr O'Connor, in his *Columbanus ad Hibernos*, written in 1810, states that he pressed a very old peasant to state what possible advantage he expected to derive from frequenting wells near 'old blasted oaks' or 'upright, unhewn stones', and to explain the meaning of spitting on, and placing rags on the branches of the surrounding trees. The old man and his companions could only explain that both they and their ancestors were always accustomed to do it, that they considered it a preservative against '*Geasa draoidecht*, i.e. the sorceries of the Druids, that their cattle were preserved by it from infectious disorders; that the *daoinimaithe*, i.e. the fairies, were kept in good humour by it; and so thoroughly persuaded were they of the sanctity of these pagan practices, that they would travel bare-headed and bare-footed from 10 to 20 miles, for the purpose of crawling on their knees around these wells, and upright stones, and oak trees, westward as the sun travels, some three times, some six, some nine, and so on, in uneven numbers, until their voluntary penances were completely fulfilled.'[27]

The reference above to wells near 'old blasted oaks' suggests that holy wells were sited near trees, and researchers have found this to often be the case. Vaughan Cornish makes several references to this fact in his book about historic thorn trees,[28] and includes this quotation on the subject from T. S. F. Paterson of the County Museum in Armagh.

In County Armagh we have many old single thorns usually called 'Fairy Thorns' or 'Lone Bushes', none of which are ever cut. To do so would bring ill luck upon the person doing the injury to the bush and possibly death. Apart from 'Fairy Thorns' we have a second class of thorns, those that overhang holy wells. These are equally venerated and it is said that when the old thorn knows its end is coming, a new thorn is born to take its place ... Usually such thorns have hundreds of rags floating from them as it is the custom to leave some portion of your clothing on a branch.

Edward O'Toole, another correspondent of Vaughan Cornish, adds:

There are about sixty Holy Wells in Co. Carlow and at, or near, most of them there is an ancient skeough (whitethorn) bush. On these bushes pilgrims to the wells were in the habit of hanging medals, crucifixes, rosary beads, or strips of cloth in acknowledgement of cures obtained there.

In County Wicklow Patrick's Bush was (and maybe still is) an old thorn tree growing above a well near Tinahely which was visited every 4 May. The pilgrims would circle the well, and on the tree hang pieces torn from their clothes.[29] This may have been done in the hope that as the cloth rotted, so the ailment for which the pilgrim sought a cure would fade away, but it may also, at a deeper level, have involved an appreciation of the tree as a symbol of renewal. If a well dried up, its 'spirit' could be moved to a nearby sacred tree. The so-called Pin Well at Arboe in County Tyrone is in fact a beech tree stuck with pins and nails and growing in a Celtic monastery graveyard.[30]

So far all the data relating to holy wells and trees found together has come from Ireland, but this is not surprising in view of the large number of holy wells there (W. G. Wood-Martin estimated that there were more than 3,000) and the strength of feeling surrounding sacred trees, which will be described more fully later in this chapter. But wells and trees were also found together elsewhere in Britain. On the Isle of Man thorn trees were sometimes planted over holy wells, one such well being actually known as Chibby Drine, or the Well of the Thorn Tree (in the parish of Kirk Malew),[31] and there was also a Chibber Unjin, or Well of the Ash-tree, where votive offerings were hung on the sacred ash-tree.[32] At a certain Scottish holy well the presence of a yew tree was vital to the successful working of the well. 'The Well of the Yew' was in Easter Ross, and before the tree was cut down the well was successful in curing a disease known as 'white swelling'.[33]

The association between holy wells and sacred trees goes back many centuries, as is indicated by the contents of a Celtic shaft-well discovered at Ashill in Norfolk. Formed of wood and 40 feet deep, it was found to contain pottery, bones, a basket and a knife, and, below 20 feet, layers of urns embedded in the leaves and nuts of the hazel tree. Anne Ross points out that 'Any examination of the corpus of early Irish literary tradition ... reveals that, not only was the hazel tree itself venerated, but its traditional association with sacred wells is fully attested', and gives examples of its importance to the Celts. The significance of the Ashill well to the people who constructed it, and their descendants, was shown by the discovery of frequently used paths leading to the place.[34] Since Celtic times, and maybe also before, the hazel tree has been a holy tree with fertility associations, and even in recent times country people still connected it with love and childbirth.[35]

A study of holy wells throughout Britain shows that they were often situated close by special trees, often thorns, and it was often the custom to hang rags on to the branches, as in Ireland, and hence the name 'Rag Well' given to some of them. This custom was not confined to Britain. In India new flags were hung on bushes beside sacred wells, and there is evidence of similar customs in Ceylon, Iran, north and west Africa, Abyssinia, and Arabia.[36] Why should holy wells and trees be so closely associated? Erich Neumann's quotation with which this chapter opens gives one interpretation: that the well represents the

A lone thorn stands beside St Anne's Well in the churchyard at Whitstone in Cornwall (left).

Rags still adorn the thorn trees around Madron holy well in Cornwall (right). This was (and may still be) a healing well, but young girls also went there in May 'to try for sweethearts'. They would drop pairs of crooked pins or small heavy objects into the water, and if they stayed together, the girl would marry her sweetheart.

female, and the tree represents the male. This does not necessarily refer to the phallic shape of the tree, since not all trees have this shape. Many are rounded, and others, like thorn trees, are relatively small. The contrast lies rather in the receptive, inward-looking nature of the well and the vital, outward-growing nature of the tree.

Standing stones are sometimes found close to holy wells, and here the womb–phallus symbolism is clearer. In Scotland a stone circle on Card's Hill in Keith parish (Banffshire) was close to the Taber Chalich (Old Wife's Well or Well of the Cailleach – note the mother goddess dedication),[37] but we do not know if the two were linked in any special ritual. At Dungiven in County Londonderry, pilgrims visiting a certain well would, after hanging rags in the bushes, visit a large stone in the nearby River Roe. They washed themselves and walked round the stone, bowing to it and saying prayers. They followed this by a ceremony in church, and ended by returning to the stone and processing around it again.[38] In Gloucestershire there is a legend that a standing stone called the Wittelstone or Wissel Stone would go down to drink at Our Lady's Well at Nether Swell when it heard Stow clock strike.[39] All the foregoing indicate close links between certain wells and standing stones, suggestive of forgotten rituals. These would be likely to involve fertility, a theme which has followed us through this discussion of holy wells. Before turning our attention to sacred trees and their significance, there is a legend which combines three of the subjects of this chapter – holy wells, the head cult, and sacred trees – in a powerful symbolic fertility image. St Melor of Brittany and Cornwall was murdered and his severed head taken by the murderer, who intended to carry it back to the saint's uncle who had ordered the killing. On the journey he became faint from thirst, and cried out for help. He was answered by St Melor's head, which told him to plant his staff in the ground. When he had done that, not only did a spring of water spout from the ground, but the staff 'took root and was turned into a most beautiful tree, and brought forth branches and fruit, and from its root an unfailing fountain began to well forth.'[40]

There is a vast amount of lore from all over the world which tells of the sacred nature of the tree. This takes many forms, and Mircea Eliade has identified seven kinds of 'vegetation cult' including 'the tree as image of the cosmos', 'the tree as centre of the world and support of the universe', 'mystical bonds between trees and men' and, most relevant in the context of this chapter, 'the tree as symbol of life, of inexhaustible fertility, of absolute reality; as related to the Great

The Holy Thorn among the abbey ruins at Glastonbury (top).
Bawming the Thorn at Appleton in 1977 (bottom).

104

Goddess or the symbolism of water; as identified with the fount of immortality', and 'the tree as symbol of the resurrection of vegetation, of spring and of the "rebirth" of the year'.[41] Even restricting our survey to Britain, there is plenty of evidence to show how important trees have always been to man, enough to fill a book.[42] Some trees were decorated annually, as at Satterthwaite in Cumbria where on Maundy Thursday the great oak by a fountain was decked with coloured rags and crockery.[43] Tree worship took many forms, and has even survived to the present day. The deep-rooted Irish thorn cult still remains, as evidenced by the occasional news report that the course of a new road has had to be diverted to avoid cutting down a sacred tree,[44] while in England the attention paid to the Holy Thorn at Glastonbury is all that remains of an English thorn cult. Until quite recently, people would gather on Old Christmas Eve (5 January) to watch the Holy Thorns flower. The bushes were mainly in Somerset and Hereford-shire, with a few in other counties.[45] In Hampshire a similar custom was followed at the Cadnam Oak at Copythorne, where on Old Christmas Eve people used to hold parties beneath the tree and watch for its first buds, which opened on Old Christmas Day.[46] Another example of the thorn cult in England which has been abandoned only in the past few years, and may yet be resurrected, is the custom of Bawming the Thorn. The first thorn on the site at Appleton near Warrington in Cheshire was, according to tradition, an offshoot of the Glastonbury Holy Thorn. For hundreds of years the tree was 'bawmed' (adorned) annually on or around Old Midsummer Day (5 July) with flowers and ribbons. The people (in later years, the children only) danced around the tree, and the ceremony was followed by sports and other amusements.[47]

As we have already seen, it was not only thorn trees that were venerated. In England the oak is the most likely species to be thought of as a sacred tree, from its traditional association with the Druids to the twentieth-century 'pilgrims' who visit the Major Oak in Sherwood Forest in Nottinghamshire. On a hot summer weekend in 1979, when we last visited the Major Oak, scores of people were trekking along the fenced-in path through the forest towards their goal, and when they got there they sat around for a few minutes before plodding back. The once-popular Oak Apple Day may also have had its roots in tree worship, though it was officially celebrated on 29 May to commemorate the day in 1660 when Charles II was restored to the throne after hiding in an oak tree. The celebration involved adorning

The Major Oak in Sherwood Forest (top).
Another venerated tree, the Great Oak at Great Yeldham in Essex. The remains of this ancient tree, believed to be over 300 years old, are carefully preserved on an island in the centre of the road where the villagers also meet to pass the time of day beneath a replacement oak planted in 1863 to commemorate the marriage of King Edward VII and Queen Alexandra, then, of course, Prince and Princess of Wales.

churches, houses and statues with oak boughs, and wearing oak leaves on one's person.[48]

A black poplar is the focal point of another tree ceremony which is still practised. Once a year, on 29 May, Arbor Day is held at Aston-on-Clun in Shropshire. Flags on poles are hung in the Arbor Tree, and left there the whole year round. Although the festival almost certainly began as a tree-worshipping ceremony, today the focus of attention has shifted from the tree to the re-enactment of an eighteenth-century wedding which takes place beneath it, the village children dressed in period costume to act out the roles of bride, groom and attendants. This was followed, in 1980 when we attended, by morris dancing, and children's maypole dancing, both beneath the Arbor Tree (and in the rain!), after which everyone walked to a nearby field and barn where a typical country fête was soon in full swing, with 'guessing the weight of the sheep' and 'welly-wanging', all watched by bemused hens.[49] It is interesting to compare the atmosphere of an unspoilt rural celebration such as this, with the overcrowding and rowdiness unfortunately now predominant at such popular festivities as May Day at Padstow.

Dancing around trees seemed to be an integral part of tree-worship, and in Devon there were special 'dancing trees' around which the people danced on certain days of the year. They even celebrated *on top of* some trees, like the Meavy Oak. Such trees were kept clipped flat on top, and at festival time a platform would be built above the tree, with steps leading up to it. A table and chairs were carried up, and a feast was held on top of the tree.[50] In parts of Wales a flower-decked birch tree would be set up for dancing beginning on St John's Day (24 June/Midsummer Day) and lasting for several days if the weather was good.[51] There is a close similarity to the custom of dancing around the maypole on May Day, a custom whose significance we shall explore more fully later in this chapter, and in Chapter 10. One last reminder of present-day tree worship is the ubiquitous Christmas tree, decorated and candlelit, without which no British child's Christmas would be complete. In fact the Christmas tree only became popular in Britain in the late nineteenth century, the idea being imported from Germany, though it is a natural development of the midwinter custom of decking the house with greenery, a reminder of the imminent arrival of spring and the coming of new life to the land.[52]

As we suggested earlier, the tree embodies fertility symbolism and this takes several forms. In one aspect it is 'the earth phallus, the male principle jutting out of the earth',[53] while 'as fruit-bearing tree of life it is female'.[54] In some parts of the world, resin from coniferous trees was regarded as the Earth Mother's menstruation,[55] which reminds us

Everyone stands still as the last flag, of St George, is raised in the Arbor Tree at Aston-on-Clun on Arbor Day.

of British legends concerning bleeding yew, elder and hawthorn trees. The most famous 'bleeding' yew is in Nevern churchyard, Dyfed, and no proper explanation has been forthcoming for the red substance

A 'bleeding yew' at Nevern.

which exudes from its trunk. It was life-blood rather than menstrual blood which flowed from a Holy Thorn being cut down at Clehonger in Herefordshire, so the story goes. The man committing the evil act was so terrified when he saw the blood coming from its trunk that he left the thorn where it was.[56] Bleeding elders are usually witches in disguise, like the famous tree near the Rollright Stones in Oxfordshire. A witch turned a king and his army into standing stones, and she herself became an elder tree. When the tree was cut during the annual Midsummer Eve ceremonies, it bled.

The Christian religion also involves fertility themes associated with trees, though these are hidden rather than explicit. The complex symbolism in the story of Adam and Eve and the Tree of Knowledge is explored by Mircea Eliade, who suggests that man was searching for the Tree of Life which bestowed immortality, but he was obstructed in his search by the serpent which may have wished to be the first to find the Tree of Life and eat its fruit.[57] Eliade tells us that 'The Tree of Life is the prototype of all miraculous plants that bring the dead to life, heal the sick, restore youth, and so on ... In Christian iconography the cross is often depicted as the Tree of Life.'[58] Erich Neumann also explores the symbolism of cross and gallows.

Adam and Eve and the serpent in the Garden of Eden (left).
The cross as the Tree of Life (right).

Here, it is evident, sacrifice, death, rebirth, and wisdom are intertwined on a new plane. Thus tree of life, cross, and gallows tree are ambivalent forms of the maternal tree. What hangs on the tree, the child of the tree mother, suffers death but receives immortality from her, who causes him to rise to her immortal heaven, where he partakes in her essence as giver of wisdom, as Sophia. Sacrifice and suffering are the prerequisites of the transformation conferred by her, and this law of dying and becoming is an essential part of the wisdom of the Great Goddess of living things, the goddess of all growth, psychic as well as physical ... Christ, hanging from the tree of death, is the fruit of suffering and hence the pledge of the promised land, the beatitude to come; and at the same time He is the tree of life as the god of the grape.[59]

Although tree worship was once widespread, and certain aspects of it still survive in Britain today, for the most part the beliefs and ceremonies are only a shadow of what once took place around the world.[60] But the surviving fertility customs linked with trees show what power the beliefs must once have held. Was the Cleveland custom,

Tree worship sometimes took strange forms, such as driving coins edgeways into the bark. One such holy tree was in Innis Maree on Loch Maree, Wester Ross, Highland Region, and so many coins were hammered into the tree that it was covered with metallic scales to a height of eight or nine feet. This devotion eventually killed it. A tree similarly adorned can still be seen in the Slieve Bloom area of County Laois.

practised until recently, of hanging animals' placentas in thorn trees a thank-offering to the tree goddess for the safe births, or simply a method of disposing of the placentas by leaving them out for winged scavengers?[61] Trees were often thought to be of value to those hoping for love and marriage. The Trysting Pine (or Kissing or Wishing Tree) on Barnham Cross Common near Thetford, in Norfolk, has acquired magical powers because its trunk has formed into a loop, and the ritual is either to pull off a cone, hold it in the right hand, put your head through the loop and make a wish, or, for couples visiting the tree, to hold hands and kiss through the loop.[62] In Hampshire it is a gypsy belief that a missing lover can be brought back by a charm repeated on three nights, the hopeful girl also having to place a piece of oak with an acorn attached to it, and a piece of ash with its 'keys', under her pillow. The words of the charm are:

> Acorn cup and ashen key,
> Bid my true love come to me –
> Between moonlight and firelight,
> Bring him over the hills tonight;
> Over the meadows, over the moor,
> Over the rivers, over the sea,
> Over the threshold and in at the door.
> Acorn cup and ashen key,
> Bring my true love back to me.[63]

Anyone wishing to know if their lover would marry them should take two acorns, one for each of the two persons concerned, and drop them in a basin of water. If they floated close together, the couple would marry, but if they separated, the relationship would not prosper and the marriage would not occur.[64] It is doubtful whether young lovers realized that in Greece and Rome the cupped acorn represented the *glans penis*.[65] Or that, when indulging in Christmas kisses under the mistletoe, the milky liquid in the berries was in olden times likened to sperm – which may be why mistletoe became revered as a sacred plant bringing fertility.[66] Mistletoe growing on an oak was the most efficacious, according to Pliny, and women wishing to conceive should carry some about with them.[67]

Couples whose togetherness was assured would, in pre-Christian times, sometimes be married beneath a sacred tree known as a Marriage Oak. Even when Christianity had become the official religion, the belief in the importance of the Marriage Oak was not always forgotten, and newly married couples would hasten to the sacred tree, dance around it and cut a cross in it.[68] A bride would often include myrtle in her bridal bouquet, for it was considered to be lucky, and would bring fertility. A myrtle sprig was also used in a marriage-divination ritual formerly practised in the English Midlands and North. Folklorist S. O. Addy instructed the curious girl as follows:

On Midsummer Eve, let a girl take a sprig of myrtle and lay it in her Prayer Book upon the words of the marriage service, 'Wilt thou take this man to be thy wedded husband?' Then let her close the book, put it under her pillow, and sleep upon it. If her lover will marry her, the myrtle will be gone in the morning, but if it remains in the book, he will not marry her.[69]

When orange-blossom was introduced into Britain it gradually took over from myrtle the role of fertility plant in the bride's bouquet, while in Norfolk the fruit of the orange was used in a strange love-charm, in which a man wishing for a girl's love would sleep all night with an orange in his armpit, next day giving it to the girl of his choice. If she ate it, her love would be his![70] Nuts were also often included somewhere in the marriage festivities, being symbols of fertility. In Devon, an old woman would meet the bride leaving church and give her a bag of hazel nuts.[71] A good nut harvest signified plenty of babies during the coming year, with double nuts meaning twins. A girl should not go nutting on a Sunday, for she would meet the Devil and have a baby before her wedding![72]

Venerable yew trees of great antiquity can be found in a number of churchyards in Britain, most of them carefully preserved and cared for, but rarely are they the focus of fertility lore. An exception is the old yew in Stoke Gabriel churchyard, Devon. Fertility is achieved for a male by walking backwards round the tree, for a female by walking forwards round it.[73]

A general rather than specific acquisition of fertility was intended by the widespread use of trees and foliage in May Day celebrations throughout Europe. In the belief that the tree-spirit would fertilize women and cattle, and make the crops grow, houses and farm buildings were decked with greenery,[74] while whole trees were cut and then re-erected in the village. Although later a pole was left permanently erected and then decorated at each year's May festivities, originally a new tree was brought each year. Since the tree embodies the newly awakened spirit of vegetation, a dead tree would hardly have the same power, and the re-use of a 'dead' pole indicated that by then the real meaning of the custom had been forgotten,[75] although as a

113

phallic symbol it could still suggest the flow of energy between cosmos and earth which the people were seeking to invoke.

The significance of the May Day festivities will be explored further in Chapter 10; meanwhile we will close this chapter by restating in Mircea Eliade's words that 'the cosmos is symbolized by a tree' and 'fertility, wealth, luck, health' are all 'concentrated in herbs or trees'[76] – hence the desire of rural people to bring the tree into the heart of their communities at the vital time when fertility and renewal were sought.

The tallest permanent maypole in England (86 feet) is at Barwick in Elmet, West Yorkshire. Note the four garlands which decorate it.

7 The agricultural cycle: preparing the ground

'And this world, too, is in transformation, bursting eggs and crawling young, corpses decomposing into earth, and life arising from swamp and muck.'

Erich Neumann, *The Great Mother*[1]

Man has always been aware of the natural cycle of birth, death and rebirth; but he has not taken the role of passive observer. In his desire for more and better food than could be obtained from the wild, he began to manipulate nature and thus was agriculture born. From then on, the preoccupation of agricultural man was with the maintenance of fertility and the arrival of sunshine and rain when needed. Even with today's high level of technology man still has no control over the weather, and farmers are still at the mercy of nature. But so far as fertility is concerned today, the practices we shall describe in this chapter have been almost entirely superseded by the application of chemicals. The disastrous effect of this on the land is becoming increasingly apparent to those who can see beyond the physical surface.

Observation of the natural cycle, together with experience, taught the first farmers how they could promote the fertility of their land and crops and livestock. They knew, however, that good crops and healthy cattle were not achieved solely by keeping the land fertile, important as that was; there were other invisible forces at work. Innumerable rituals were followed as men attempted to reinforce these subtle forces and to influence them to work in their favour: rituals to encourage the return of the life-giving sun, rituals to energize the sprouting seed, rituals to cause the rain to fall ... Some of these rituals have survived to the present day, but now their original significance is forgotten and they represent simply the quaint rural customs of past ages. In this and the following chapter we hope to rediscover the concepts which provided that original impetus.

Rain is one of the necessities for a successful crop, but all too often it falls when unwanted and is absent when the need is desperate. The vital fluid from above, sent by the sky father to fertilize the earth mother, sometimes had to be encouraged to fall, and rain-making ceremonies are known from many parts of the world. The Aborigines of the Albert District of New South Wales in Australia used a special 'rain-stone' which, because of striations in the stone, looked like solidified rain. When they needed rain, the natives held a ceremony from which all females were excluded (because the rain was thought of as a male substance, produced by a male god?), with talking, dancing, singing, and 'mystical performances'. Finally the rain-stone was taken by the chief from its covering of leaves and rag, and buried in the sand. The Aborigines showed Mr W. H. J. Slee, a Government Inspector of Mines who attended a rain-making ceremony in the early 1880s, the marks of a high flood in the creek, which they said had occurred after one of their earlier ceremonies.[2]

If a 1981 Press report is to be believed, the inhabitants of the Gaoligan mountain region in Yunnan, China, do not need to resort to rain-making ceremonies – they just shout! A group of pools at the foot of the mountain is known as 'the mysterious lakes' because

The North American Zuni Indians performing a rain dance, photographed in 1899. In 1963, the Cloud Clan from the Ute Indian Reservation in south-west Colorado performed a ceremonial dance when snow was lacking on the ski slopes. Two feet of snow fell in the following three days.

'Whenever anyone speaks in a loud voice at the side of the lake, heavy rain immediately follows. The louder the speaker, the heavier the rain and the longer the person speaks, the longer the rain lasts.' A local Communist Party boss who was sceptical of the reports went to the lakes and shouted, whereupon in less than a minute it began to rain. One theory to explain this strange phenomenon is that the air is so wet that the slightest vibration can cause rain to fall.[3]

Living in a region so short of water, the Australian Aborigines could not use water in their rain-making ceremonies, but in the British Isles such ceremonies often involved water sprinkling, perhaps with the intention of encouraging the rain by example. Anyone standing on the stepping-stones in Tarn Dulyn in the Snowdonia area of North Wales could be sure of rain before nightfall if he threw water on to the farthest stepping-stone.[4] In the Hebrides, the Water Cross on the island of Uist used to be raised when rain was needed, and lowered

A witchcraft ritual to produce rain, illustrated in Ulrich Molitor, *De Laniis et Phitonicis Mulieribus*, 1489.

when the people had sufficient.[5] Of course witches were believed to be able to produce rain at will, but it was said that they usually did this as an evil act and rarely because the farmers needed it. The cutting or burning of ferns (or in some other areas heather) was widely believed to cause rain. This belief is illustrated in a letter written by Philip Herbert, third Earl of Pembroke and Lord Chamberlain to Charles I, in 1636, and addressed to 'my very loving friend the High Sheriff of the county of Stafford'.

Sir,
    His Majesty taking notice of an opinion entertained in Staffordshire that the burning of Ferne doth draw downe rain, and being desirous that the country and himself may enjoy fair weather as long as he remains in those parts, his Majesty hath commanded me to write to you, to cause all burning of Ferne to bee forborne untill his Majesty be passed this country. Wherein, not doubting but the consideration of their own interest, as well as of his Ma[jes]ties, will invite the country to a ready observance of this his Ma[jes]ties command,
                I rest your very loving friend,
                    Pembroke and Montgomery[6]

The nature of the weather on certain days was believed to indicate future weather or crop prospects, and even today if it rains on St Swithin's Day, 15 July, some people fear that there will be forty days of bad weather. But apple-growers welcomed rain on that day, or on 29 June (St Peter's Day), for this meant that the saints were watering the orchards and there would be a good crop.[7] Without realizing it, people today still participate in rain-making ceremonies when they perform some of the old customs which include ritual water-sprinkling, and some examples of these will be given in Chapter 11.

Farmers also relied on springs and wells for their water supply, and both in veneration of the miraculous source, and in hopes of ensuring its continuance, they frequently performed special rituals there. One which was once widespread and still survives strongly in Derbyshire today is the custom of well-dressing, when the wells are decorated with flowers, as described in Chapter 6.

Important as rain is to the farmer, in Britain at least it is rarely absent for long, and there is usually more than enough. Despite famous drought years like 1976 which stay in the memory, it is a fact that in Britain the watercourses are rarely low, the springs and wells rarely fail, and few weeks pass without rain. The rain gods truly favour Britain, which probably explains why there are not many British rain-making rituals. But when we consider the maintenance of the fertility of the land, we must forget the gods for a while, because the basics of fertility are the responsibility of the farmer and no one else. That farmers in past centuries were aware of this responsibility is demonstrated by the Irish habit of siting the dungheap in front of the house, or even collecting dung at one end of the living-room, as they sometimes did in remote farmhouses up to 200 years ago. To them, their muck symbolized the farm's fertility. In some parts of Ireland, a rowan sprig was stuck into the heap on May Eve to protect the farm.[8]

It is not possible to describe in detail all the farmer's practical methods of maintaining the fertility of the land, but a reading of books dealing with the subject of traditional agriculture shows clearly that our ancestors were very conscientious farmers, and followed the proverb: 'A farmer should live as though he were going to die tomorrow; but he should farm as though he were going to live for ever.' As a result, most land, despite having been farmed for centuries, is still fertile and productive near the end of the twentieth century. Whether it will remain so for long is less certain, since many farmers today both live *and* farm as though they were going to die tomorrow. Maximization of profit is the goal, and the well-being of the land has been forgotten. Only a few island or shoreline farmers today know the value of seaweed as a fertilizer, for example. Yet in times past, it was widely used. There were special rituals designed to produce a good 'crop' of seaweed, and in the island of Lewis (Western Isles) in the seventeenth century the people would gather on All Hallows night at the church of St Mulvay, then one would wade into the water carrying a cup of ale. He cried: 'Shony, I give you this cup of ale, hoping that you will be so kind as to send us plenty of sea-ware for enriching our ground the ensuing year'; and poured the ale into the sea. Afterwards the people went back to the church and doused a candle burning on the altar. The night ended with drinking, singing and dancing. No one knows anything about the sea-god they invoked, Shony. Later, after this ceremony had been repressed, people used to gather to invoke Briannuil to 'send a strong north wind to drive plenty sea-ware ashore.'[9] At some seaweed rituals on the west coast of Scotland, men would walk into the sea and chant

> O God of the sea,
> Put weed in the drawing wave,
> To enrich the ground,
> To shower on us food.[10]

In the Hebrides, Maundy Thursday was 'the Day of the Big Porridge' when, if the supply of seaweed was not sufficient for the farmers' needs, a large pot of specially rich porridge was made and then poured from selected headlands into parts of the sea known to be fertile seaweed grounds, accompanied by chants and rhymes. This should only be done in stormy weather, and the result was, the people hoped, a good crop of 'sea-ware'.[11] In Aberdeenshire as late as the nineteenth century, the farmers used to gather the first load of seaweed, or 'waar', on New Year's morning, take it home, and place a small amount at each door of the farmstead, before throwing the rest into the fields, making sure that each field had a share. Presumably this custom indicated their intentions for the year, to maintain their farm's fertility.[12]

Another widespread custom which is today unknown was marling, and marlpits can still be found indicated by name on Ordnance Survey maps. The mineral-rich clay dug out of the pits was spread on the land

Hebrideans on the island of Lewis in the Outer Hebrides gathering fucus (seaweed) along Loch Seaforth, photographed in April 1938.

as a fertilizer, and the craft had its own customs. The completion of marling might be celebrated by dancing and festivities, or even with fertility-related customs like maypole dancing, as took place at Little Crosby in Lancashire in July 1712.[13]

Besides the practical activities of making dung-heaps, spreading seaweed, and marling, there were rituals of a more symbolic nature designed to direct the mental energies of the participants towards those positive attitudes which were known to be necessary for the well-being of plant and animal. The scattering of substances across the fields, particularly blood (often let from living cattle) and ashes (often from ceremonial bonfires), played a significant part in such rituals, and later we will discuss them in detail. But first here are a few other customs of a similar nature. In Ireland, a fistful of salt was sometimes sprinkled on a field in order to keep the soil fertile,[14] while in Wales, farmers living near Scyrrid Vawr, or the Holy Mountain, near Abergavenny in Gwent, would sprinkle a handful of soil taken from

An islander from South Uist in the Outer Hebrides shows how he used a primitive foot spade to prepare a 'lazy bed'. The soil from trenches was thrown over seaweed gathered from the shore and spread on the ground. Photographed in April 1928.

the summit of the mountain on to their fields after sowing.[15] Again in Ireland, the first milk from a newly calved cow would be allowed to fall on the ground 'for those who might need it',[16] the farmer perhaps wishing to propitiate the Little People or other invisible entities who could, if they wished, create havoc on the farm. In Scotland it was the Glaistig who had to be humoured. In Glen Duror of Appin, in Argyll (Strathclyde), she would prevent the cows from suckling their calves at night, and so every evening for several generations a little milk was poured into a hollow in a stone, known as the Clach na Glaistig (the Glaistig's Stone).[17] Still in Scotland, oblations of milk were poured on the hills in Gairloch, Ross and Cromarty (Highland), and offerings made to the *fridean*, supernatural beings living under or inside rocks and considered to be fertility spirits.[18]

Another custom which may originally have been followed with the intention of making offerings to supernatural beings was practised in parts of Wales. When the fruit was gathered in the orchards, a few (three, seven or nine) apples or pears or plums would be left on each tree, to ensure a good crop next year.[19] In the north of Scotland, a mouse was buried under an apple tree, and a cat under a pear tree, to ensure good fruit crops.[20]

Throughout the year, on the appropriate date, ceremonial bonfires were lit, and these fire festivals were all concerned with various aspects of fertility. There were eight of these significant dates, and they fall into two groups of four. Four of them were related to the movements of the moon and four to the sun. The lunar fire festivals were Samhain (1 November), Imbolc/Oimelc (1 February), Beltane (1 May) and Lugnasad/Lammas (1 August), and those which were derived from the sun's apparent movement were on or near 22 December (the Winter Solstice), 21 March (the Spring Equinox), 22 June (the Summer Solstice), and 23 September (the Autumn Equinox). Thus throughout the year there was a balanced interlocking of the feminine – lunar – earth mother forces with those of the masculine – solar – sky father, a balance which is sadly lacking in today's intensely aggressive patriarchal society. The painstaking surveys of Professor Thom have shown that many stone circles and their attendant alignments, some as old as 4,000 years, are positioned to mark some of these sacred dates.[21] Nearly all the fire ceremonies referred to throughout this book fall on or near one of these significant dates, and so we hope the above notes will help readers to place these seasonal events within the annual cycle.

The summer solstice was still being celebrated in Ireland in the late eighteenth century, as this traveller discovered.

At the house where I was entertained, in the summer of 1782, it was told me that we should see at midnight the most singular sight in Ireland, which was the lighting of fires in honour of the sun. Accordingly, exactly at midnight, the fires began to appear; and, going up to the leads of the house, which had a widely-extended view, I saw, on a radius of thirty miles all around, the fires burning on every eminence. I learned from undoubted authority that the people danced round the fires, and at the close went through these fires, and made their sons and daughters, together with their cattle, pass the fire; and the whole was conducted with religious solemnity. [22]

Traditionally, flaming cartwheels, bound with straw and pitch, were sent bowling down hillsides in order to quicken the powers of the dying sun. In the Vale of Glamorgan, a blazing wheel was trundled downhill on Midsummer Day. If the flames were extinguished before it reached

This old photograph shows the Baal Fire at Whalton, Northumberland, which is lit on 4 July (Old Midsummer Eve) when it grows dark. As part of the ceremony, the village children dance in a ring around the fire.

the bottom, a poor harvest was expected, but if the flames continued to burn vigorously, then the harvest would be abundant.[23] Similar practices were widely followed throughout the whole of Europe, usually associated with a Midsummer bonfire ceremony, the bonfire being lit on one of the numerous sacred high points which were focuses of the earth energy system.[24]

Personal fertility and good fortune were acquired by the hazardous act of jumping over a blazing bonfire, though it often seems to have been sufficient to dance or jump over glowing embers, as was the custom at the bonfire lit at Fortingall in Perthshire on 11 November.[25] It has been suggested that at the ceremonial bonfires 'women used to stride over the fire, exposing their vulvas to the beneficial influence of the flame, and blessing it with their own power', since the human genitals were believed to have magical powers to avert evil and misfortune.[26]

The fire and smoke of the bonfire were also used to protect and fertilize the crops and cattle. The fire 'destroyed the powers hostile to man, purified the air, and allowed man and beast and vegetation to thrive and become fertile.'[27] In the Orkney Islands, blazing heather from the Johnsmas (Midsummer) bonfires was carried among the cattle in the sheds, to keep them healthy and help the cows to keep producing calves. Blazing torches were also carried round the fields and houses.[28] In Scotland generally, the cornfields were blessed at Midsummer when burning wooden torches were carried round them in sunwise procession.[29] Smoke from the 11 May (Old May Eve) bonfires on the Isle of Man passed across fields, cattle and horses to purify them, or a bit of gorse was lit in each field, and on St John's Eve or Midsummer Eve (23 June) bonfires were lit on the hilltops and blazing wheels rolled downhill. Men and boys leapt over the flames, and cattle were driven over or between fires to keep them healthy. Again smoke was directed over the cornfields, and torches of blazing furze or gorse carried round the cattle.[30] Similar customs were practised in the Irish Republic and Northern Ireland, barren cattle especially being driven through the Midsummer fires.[31] In Mevagh parish in north Donegal, coals taken from the Midsummer fires were thrown into the fields to ensure good crops, and particularly to protect the potatoes from blight. In the Kilrea area of east Londonderry, the piece of wood put in the field was called 'the flower of the bonfire'.[32] In the Aran Islands also, blazing bushes from the St John's Eve bonfires were thrown into the potato gardens and rye fields for luck.[33]

In one Irish St John's Eve fire ceremony held in the first half of the nineteenth century, a variant on the custom of driving cattle through the flames was witnessed.

When the fire burned for some hours, and got low, an indispensable part of the ceremony commenced. Every one present of the peasantry passed through it, and several children were thrown across the sparkling embers; while a wooden frame of some 8 feet long, with a horse's head fixed to one end, and a large white sheet thrown over it, concealing the wood and the man on whose head it was carried, made its appearance. This was greeted with loud shouts as the '*white horse*'; and having been safely carried by the skill of its bearer several times through the fire with a bold leap, it pursued the people, who ran screaming and laughing in every direction. I asked what the horse was meant for, and was told it represented all cattle.[34]

The link between the horse and fertility is explored more fully in Chapter 11, and may throw some light on this unusual Irish bonfire custom.

Throughout England and Wales, too, bonfires were lit to promote fertility. In Herefordshire, south-west Worcestershire, and Gwent, bonfires were lit on Twelfth Night in the wheat fields and the crops were 'wassailed' with much shouting and toasts of cider. A good supper followed, and later in the evening a strange ritual took place in the cowshed. The cattle and oxen were toasted, and a large plum cake with a hole in it was hung on the horn of one of the oxen. He was tickled or drenched with cider to make him throw it off, and if it fell forward, there would be a good harvest.[35] In Herefordshire another fire custom was widely practised a few days earlier, on New Year's Day. A small 'bush' of hawthorn twigs was taken out into the earliest sown wheat field very early in the morning and burnt in a fire of straw and bushes. While the fire was burning, a new 'bush' was made, which hung in the farmhouse kitchen until the next New Year's Day. Sometimes cider was poured over the new bush after its ends had been scorched in the fire. At Brinsop, the burning bush was carried across the crops. The farmers believed that the ceremony of 'burning the bush' was essential for the welfare of the crop, and the shape of the bush suggests it was originally a sun symbol.[36] In Worcestershire, a crown of blackthorn was made early on New Year's morning, baked in the oven, and then completely burnt in the nearest cornfield and the ashes scattered over the wheat.[37]

The practice of carrying the purifying fire around the fields and orchards and of scattering ashes to promote fertility was widespread in

Burning the Clavie at Burghead (top).
The Allendale tar-barrel ceremony, photographed in 1965 (bottom).

126

Britain and Europe,[38] and it has been suggested that this custom may be a relic of the time when the land was fired before crops were sown.[39] In parts of Wales the ashes of the Yule log[40] were kept until the seeds were sown, and then mixed with them and thus scattered on the fields, to bring a good crop.[41] There are even some fire festivals still held today where charred pieces of wood are prized as 'lucky' tokens. On 11 January at Burghead in Grampian, Burning the Clavie takes place, when a blazing half-barrel of tar and wood on a pole is carried round the boundaries of the old town. Pieces of charred wood are handed to householders to bring them good luck in the coming year. The procession ends at a mound on a headland known as Doorie Hill, where the clavie is placed on a stone pillar and the fire built up to a large blaze. Later it is beaten out by the clavie team who scatter burning fragments in all directions while the crowd scramble for pieces of the embers.[42] On 31 December at Allendale in Northumberland 'guisers' carry tubs on their heads around the town. These are made from a half-barrel and filled with blazing wood and shavings. At midnight the guisers meet in the square to light a bonfire.[43] There are a number of large communal bonfires on New Year's Eve in Scotland, and at Stonehaven in Kincardineshire the young men whirl balls of incandescent material round their heads on the end of wire ropes. These are perhaps similar in purpose to the blazing cartwheels already described.[44]

The use of blood in fertility rites was at one time widespread, and possibly indicates that in even earlier times human or animal sacrifices were performed. It might seem that this is an unconvincing way to illustrate harmony between man and earth, but the attitudes of today's largely urban population (with their plastic-wrapped and pre-sliced meats), carefully protected from the harsher realities, must be very different from those earlier peoples to whom birth and death were everyday events. The early farmers must have felt that they had good reason to perform sacrifices. They were part of the farmers' efforts to perpetuate the cycle of death and rebirth: by giving their life-spirit, the sacrificed person or animal would enrich the natural life, and thus strengthen the vegetation and crops. Although we have little direct folklore evidence of human sacrifice in Britain, it was probably performed in the distant past, possibly in the bonfire ceremonies just described, just as it was performed elsewhere in the world, even as recently as the 1830s among the Pawnee Indians.[45]

There are British customs which hint of sacrifice. In the

Worcestershire hopfields, on the last day of hop picking, the foreman and a woman were buried under hops in one of the baskets in which they were collected, and then the two were resurrected by being tipped out.[46] This may have been a relic of a sacrifice aimed at ensuring a good harvest next year, similar to the ritual of the Corn Maiden, which we shall describe fully in the next chapter, and which is most likely all that remains of a human sacrificial ritual. Other examples are given in Chapter 9, which deals specifically with ritual sacrifice. Archaeologists have found evidence suggestive of prehistoric sacrifice, for example at long barrows in Wiltshire where skulls were discovered which showed severe injury almost certainly inflicted before death.[47]

In Britain, sacrifice became 'toned down' to blood-letting, which was thought to be nearly as efficacious since blood contains the life-essence. So shedding blood does not signify taking life but giving it, or, as folklorist and author of a book on sacrifice, E. O. James, put it: blood is 'a kind of soul-substance responsible for the phenomenon of life'.[48] Although human sacrifice was discontinued, animal sacrifice was still practised until quite recently. On the Isle of Man there were cases in the nineteenth century of farmers with sick cattle sacrificing one in the hope that this would cause the others to be restored to health. A contemporary description from Maughold of a sacrifice made in 1853 reads: 'The calf was dragged to an eminence not far from the highway, a large quantity of peat and straw was provided, and, a light having been applied, the calf and pyre were consumed.'[49] A custom of fishermen in Scotland was to kill a goat before they set sail, 'thereby hoping for the better Successe',[50] but it is not clear how widespread this custom was. Considering how often fishermen used to go to sea, it would have been quite expensive in goats, and was probably only performed on certain occasions, or when the signs indicated that there would be a poor catch.

Memories of animal sacrifice linger on in a number of traditional customs. Some indicate that especial importance was attached to the head of the sacrificed beast,[51] while others, like the Lincolnshire Haxey Hood Game, also demonstrate the importance of bulls. The bull, so sexually energetic, was a particularly potent source of fertility, and just as he could fertilize cows, so his blood could fertilize the earth. The bull may have symbolized 'the masculine power of nature'.[52] At Haxey, in the winter, men chase the 'hood' in a very rough kind of football. The 'hood' is a length of thick rope encased in leather, and may originally have been the head of a bull sacrificed in an agricultural

The Haxey Hood Game takes place on 6 January (Old Christmas Day). A procession led by the Fool makes its way to a cross base near the church, and there he makes a welcoming speech (shown here). A fire is lit behind him as he speaks (for the significance of this, see Chapter 9), and after 'Smoking the Fool' the crowd makes its way to a field where the game begins. The Boggans (the King Boggan is seen here, carrying a willow wand as badge of office) try to prevent the Hoods (the Fool holds one in the photograph) from being carried away to other villages, and the battle rages for two or more hours. There are several pointers in the twentieth-century ceremonies to a pagan fertility rite.

fertility ritual. Or, as a fertility symbol, it may have represented the bull's most vital organ, the penis.[53]

It was usually the blood of cattle which was used to fertilize the earth. Irish farmers used to drive their cattle into the prehistoric forts on May Eve and there bleed them, taste the blood, and pour the rest on the earth.[54] The blood-letting of horses and oxen was at one time regularly performed on 26 December (St Stephen's Day) to keep them healthy during the coming year.[55] Although no mention is made of the blood being used to fertilize the earth, this may have been done originally, and later omitted when its significance was forgotten, the focus of the ritual being turned to the animal being bled. The Kingsteignton ram-roasting feast, already mentioned in Chapter 3, also originally had blood-letting as part of the ritual. The ram's blood was offered to a river god to increase the water supply.[56]

Although human sacrifice has long since died out in Britain, and probably also animal sacrifice and blood-letting (though who knows what rituals may still be secretly practised in remote agricultural communities?), the following 1965 report from an English newspaper shows that the primitive urge to sacrifice has not been completely lost!

An effigy of Mr Fred Peart, Minister of Agriculture, was burned yesterday by Mayfield farmers on one of a chain of bonfires due to be lit at dusk across East Sussex. They built the fire on a hill near the village. The effigy, dressed in a black coat, striped trousers and a bowler hat, was placed on top; and as it burned the farmers fired their shotguns at it.[57]

The first positive action to be taken in the annual round of crop growing is ploughing the earth, so preparing it to receive the seed. This disturbance of the Earth Mother for man's own purposes was a significant act and needed to be accompanied by the correct propitiatory rituals. The practice of making offerings of food and drink at the start of ploughing was probably once widespread, but few records now survive. In Aberdeenshire in the nineteenth century, special oaten bread was baked and some given to the horses in the field being ploughed after harvest, or, as in Aboyne parish in the same county, a glass of whisky was poured over the plough and a piece of bread and cheese wrapped in paper was fastened to the beam of the plough, with strict instructions from the farmer that it should not be touched but should be allowed to fall off naturally, or be eaten by the dogs.[58] Sometimes the offering was put in the furrow or thrown on to the field. The custom was called 'streeking the plough',[59] and was the northern counterpart of the English Plough Monday festival, described later in this chapter.

An old English charm for the fertility of the land and the accompanying ritual which have survived show how special attention was paid to the plough. Fennel, incense, hallowed soap and salt were to be rubbed on the wood of the plough, and seed placed upon it. The relevant part of the chant continues:

> Erce, Erce, Erce, Earth Mother,
> may the Almighty Eternal Lord
> grant you fields to increase and flourish,
> fields fruitful and healthy,
> shining harvest of shafts of millet,
> broad harvests of barley ...[60]

To early man, ploughing had a strong sexual significance, as we have already suggested in Chapter 1. Erich Neumann succinctly states it: 'The sexual union with the soil that is a constant feature of

Ploughing in the fourteenth century, an illustration from the Luttrell Psalter.

agricultural fertility rituals is based on the identity of the woman with earth and furrow, of the man with the plow. The nude recumbent goddess is the earth itself.'[61] Bronze Age rock carvings discovered in Scandinavia illustrate the theme, and that shown here is particularly clear. It shows a man and ox-team ploughing their third furrow, and it is here interpreted by Dr P. V. Glob.

It is obvious that he is engaged in the first ploughing of the year to awaken the earth's fruitfulness after the sleep of the winter with the phallus of the plough, the ploughshare ... The man's enormous phallus and the highly exaggerated reproductive organs of the oxen speak for themselves. The branch is a 'may tree', a feature of the spring fertility cult.[62]

The depiction of ploughing the third furrow ties in with a custom which was noted in Uppland, Sweden, in the nineteenth century, where three special furrows were ploughed on the first day of the spring sowing.[63]

Today the plough rituals are much more demure than those

A prehistoric rock carving from Litsleby in Scandinavia shows a man ploughing.

recorded on the rocks of Scandinavia, and all that remains is the blessing of the plough in church on Plough Sunday, which still happens today in some places in Britain. Plough Monday (the first Monday after 6 January) used to be the important day, because this was when work was begun again on the farms after the Twelve Days of Christmas, and the ploughing was the next major task to be undertaken. On Plough Monday, until the beginning of this century, a decorated plough would be dragged around, accompanied by 'plough witches' or young people in fancy dress. They demanded gifts of food, drink or money, and if these were refused they would roughly plough up the victim's front garden. The original intention behind the jollifications may have been to frighten away the evil spirits from the land, and so leave the ground pure and ready for the new crop.[64] Once these ploughing rituals had been performed, the spring or autumn ploughing could proceed, and the soil be prepared to receive the seed. In the next chapter we shall follow the agricultural cycle as the seed is sown, is encouraged to grow, and the crop finally harvested.

8 The agricultural cycle: from seed-time to harvest

'Who is nearer the truth? The old school type of farmer with his near-veneration for the land as a living partner who must be nursed and humoured? Or the modern farmer who treats the land as an inert medium into which he can pour chemicals with impunity?'

George Ewart Evans, *The Pattern Under the Plough*[1]

There is little doubt that ancient man's awareness of natural rhythms was far greater than is generally realized or acknowledged. The following viewpoint is still widely accepted.

To the primitive savage, with his short memory and imperfect means of marking the flight of time, a year may well have been so long that he failed to recognize it as a cycle at all, and watched the changing aspects of earth and heaven with a perpetual wonder, alternately delighted and alarmed, elated and cast down, according as the vicissitudes of light and heat, of plant and animal life, ministered to his comfort or threatened his existence. In autumn when the withered leaves were whirled about the forest by the nipping blast, and he looked up at the bare boughs, could he feel sure that they would ever be green again? As day by day the sun sank lower in the sky, could he be certain that the luminary would ever retrace his heavenly road? Even the waning moon, whose pale sickle rose thinner and thinner every night over the rim of the eastern horizon, may have excited in his mind a fear lest, when it had wholly vanished, there should be moons no more.[2]

Sowing the seed, an illustration from the fourteenth-century Luttrell Psalter.

135

That is Sir J. G. Frazer's patronizing view of our forefathers, as printed in his *Golden Bough*, the first edition of which was published in 1891. It is almost laughable in the light of today's growing knowledge of early man's sensitivity to the earth's ever-changing energy currents, and the cyclical movements of the heavenly bodies and their influences on terrestrial life (on which subjects more will be said in Chapter 12). Instead of always trying to belittle early man's beliefs by assuming that he had a naïve mind with no more grasp of life's mysteries than a child, we should instead examine his beliefs with an open mind and try to see whether they might not, in fact, have been based on valid experience and wisdom.

One possible misinterpretation of the beliefs of prehistoric men has arisen in the modern attempts to explain why they were apparently interested in the movements of the stars and planets, so interested that they erected thousands of ingenious stone markers which aligned with natural features on the horizon or distant standing stones and which enabled them to predict coming celestial events. The widely believed interpretation is that they needed a calendar so that they would know when to perform the annual agricultural tasks, but, as we have already remarked in our book *The Secret Country*, this idea is based on a lack of understanding of 'natural man'. There is folklore evidence that our ancestors have always relied on nature's signs to tell them when to sow the seed. The size of elm leaves showed when barley and kidney beans should be sown, the elm at one time being a familiar tree in the English countryside, now unfortunately decimated due to Dutch elm disease which spread rapidly through trees weakened by pollution. The traditional knowledge was perpetuated by means of a catchy rhyme:

> When the elmen leaf is as big as a mouse's ear,
> Then to sow barley never fear;
> When the elmen leaf is as big as an ox's eye,
> Then says I, 'Hie, boys! Hie!'
> When elm leaves are as big as a shilling,
> Plant kidney beans, if to plant 'em you're willing;
> When elm leaves are as big as a penny,
> You *must* plant kidney beans if you mean to have any.[3]

Early men read the countryside in a way that we cannot today, and they could, from the progress of the hedgerow plants, judge the likely success of their own crops. For instance, in Wales it was believed that a fine crop of mistletoe indicated a fine crop of corn.[4]

Between the sowing of the seed and the harvesting of the crop, the whole community, who all depended on a successful harvest, performed many rituals to encourage the crops to grow. One of the most widespread in former ages, but not so today, was the ceremonial coupling of male and female in the fields at springtime. This has been interpreted by all authorities as imitative magic, or 'laying the fields open to the workings of fertility'.[5] We suggest an alternative interpretation, that by experience it was known and accepted that the energy emitted by the participants in an act of sexual union would supplement and encourage the flow of natural energy inherent in the land, and thereby promote crop growth. One couple would have a

A Bronze Age 'cult-disc' from Maltegaard in Denmark. The carved design shows a man and woman about to embrace. Behind them is a tree, between them a hole possibly symbolizing the earth. They are surrounded by a 'twiggy' circular design which may represent foliage. The whole seems to depict the ritual outdoor coupling described in the text.

small effect; many couples would have a much greater effect. Mircea Eliade states that 'as many couples as possible' used to mate in the fields at this time.[6]

The same controversial interpretation can be applied to all the rituals from this time of the year which are concerned with crop growth. Sir J. G. Frazer in *The Golden Bough* paints a persuasive picture of 'primitive man', 'led astray by his ignorance of the true causes of things', believing that if he imitated nature's actions, then by a 'secret sympathy' Nature herself would leap into action and order the plants to grow, the sun to shine, the rain to fall.[7] We can now see that humanity does interact with the planet on two levels. As a man thinks so he will act and thereby bring about certain conditions in the material world. On a subtler but no less effective level current experiments are showing that the mind can have a very strong and direct influence on physical events. The bending of metal, control of plant growth and molecular movements are becoming well attested, despite the protests of sceptical materialists (see Chapter 12). If we consider the rituals that were performed, it is evident that they all involved concentration of mental and emotional energies. This could be brought about by dancing or other continuous bodily movement, by verbal repetition of set chants or verses, or other suitable methods. Those who have attended the re-enactment of a traditional custom will know that a powerful atmosphere can still be produced. This happens at Padstow on 1 May when the compelling music, the ritual movements of the dancers, and the excitement of the watchers combine to create a charged emotional atmosphere (see Chapter 10 for details). Energy is undoubtedly produced at such events, and where sexual pastimes are or were involved, the energy is at its most powerful. Hence the sexual element of many traditional customs, as Chapters 10 and 11 will demonstrate. But it is, of course, impossible to prove that the energy so produced ever had any positive effect on the crops. Just as traditional anthropologists cannot *prove* that 'imitative magic' was being performed, neither can we *prove* that harmonious energies were being produced. The interpretation of traditional customs and rituals rests with the individual, according to his beliefs and knowledge of current research. At this point it will be appropriate to describe some rituals performed to encourage crop growth.

Some crop growth rituals seem to incorporate both imitation and energy production. One is skipping, said to be 'an ancient magical game associated with the sowing and upspringing of the seed in

Springtime',[8] and still practised on Shrove Tuesday at Scarborough in North Yorkshire where men, women and children gather by the shore in the afternoon to skip together. Other regular skipping customs, practised around England, and described by Christina Hole in her

If Morris dancing was originally a fertility ritual, aimed at producing energy to help crop growth, that such dancing should be performed at the time of the May festivities is entirely appropriate. However, the institution of a new 'traditional custom' is unexpected these days. Here the South Shropshire Morris Men dance to greet the dawn on 1 May on top of the Long Mynd near Church Stretton, a 'tradition' which is only four or five years old. We photographed them in 1979. As the dancing began, the snow started to fall – spring had come!

British Folk Customs, have now died out. Some dances, such as Morris dancing, may also originally have had a similar significance, as too may the act of jumping over a bonfire, as already described in the last chapter.

A curious custom called 'heaving' or 'lifting' was once widespread in north-west and mid-west England and parts of Wales, but has now completely died out. Thomas Loggan described the procedure in a letter written in 1799.

I was sitting alone last Easter Tuesday at breakfast at the Talbot at Shrewsbury, when I was surprised by the entrance of all the female servants of the house handing in an arm-chair, lined with white, and decorated with ribbons and favours of different colours. I asked them what they wanted? Their answer was, they came to *heave* me. It was the custom of the place on that morning, and they hoped I would take a seat in their chair. It was impossible not to comply with a request very modestly made, and to a set of nymphs in their best apparel, and several of them under twenty. I wished to see all the ceremony, and seated myself accordingly. The group then lifted me from the ground, turned the chair about, and I had the felicity of a salute from each. I told them I supposed there was a fee due upon the occasion, and was answered in the affirmative; and, having satisfied the damsels in this respect, they withdrew to *heave* others.[9]

It was the tradition that on Easter Monday the men did the heaving, and on Easter Tuesday it was the women's turn. In Herefordshire and Shropshire, water from a specially wetted posy of flowers was sprinkled on the feet of the person lifted. The custom was not always performed in such a delicate way as described by Mr Loggan. In the more industrial areas, especially the towns, it was often a boisterous exercise performed in the streets without a chair and without the agreement of the victim, and many people stayed behind locked doors until midday, at which time the lifting must cease. The custom began to die out in the mid nineteenth century, perhaps because of widespread disapproval, which is illustrated by a court case from Norton in Cheshire in 1883. As reported in a northern newspaper,

A case illustrating the remarkable survival of an old Cheshire custom was heard before the Norton magistrates the other day. The prosecutor, William Pullen, charged Thomas Lawton with being in his house for an unlawful purpose. Defendant entered Mr Pullen's house, and said he had come to lift his wife, and two men followed defendant to the garden-gate. Prosecutor told defendant to get out, or he would kick him out. He would not allow any one to take such liberties. Defendant thereupon became very abusive. It was stated that defendant was endeavouring to carry out an old Cheshire custom. The men lifted women on Easter Monday, and women lifted men on Easter Tuesday. The magistrates informed defendant he must apologise and pay the costs.[10]

'Lifting' at Easter-time.

From the actions performed, heaving presumably began as a ritual to promote crop growth, but as often happened, it was adopted by the Christian Church and was latterly explained as a commemoration of the Easter resurrection. In Herefordshire the heaving party on entering a house would sing 'Jesus Christ is risen again' before performing the ritual.[11]

There are other crop growth rituals which incorporate or wholly consist of Christian practices. One is the custom of Beating the Bounds which still sometimes takes place at Rogationtide (in the fifth week after Easter). A clue to the nature of the custom comes from the word 'Rogation' which is from the Latin *rogare* meaning 'to ask or beseech'. The processions still held at this time combine the annual walking of the parish boundaries in order to fix them in people's minds (not so important today, now that good maps have been made), and asking God's blessing on the crops. By the sea, where fishing is important, the ceremony focuses on the boats and the sea rather than on the fields. Originally the perambulation would have had a ritual and psychic importance, not understood today, and may have been intended to spread and direct the vitalizing energies out to the extremities of the domain.[12]

Corn-showing was a custom which incorporated Christian blessing and pagan propitiatory offering. It was formerly practised on Easter Sunday around the Welsh border, only dying out at the end of the last century. H. H. Wood described the custom as he knew it in Herefordshire.

It was the custom at Lulham, in the parish of Madley, and also at White House, St Margaret's, for the bailiff to proceed on the afternoon of Easter Sunday to a wheat field on the farm. Plum cake was provided, and cider in wooden bottles, and consumed by the families of the workmen, and any neighbours who chose to attend. A small piece of cake was buried in the nearest part of the field, and then, a little cider being poured on it, they wished the master a good crop. The custom was discontinued about thirty years ago, when owing to the importation of the wheat from abroad, the crop had no longer so much importance, and also it gave rise to a noisy assemblage on Easter Sunday.[13]

In some places the participants would join hands and walk across the field, saying

> Every step a reap, every reap a sheaf,
> And God send the master a good harvest.[14]

Or, in Gwent where the custom was called 'walking the wheat', they would say

> A bit for God, a bit for man,
> And a bit for the fowls of the air

as they buried a little piece of cake, ate a little, and threw some into the air.[15]

In Herefordshire, some apple orchards were also visited, and cake and cider buried there.[16] This surely must have links with the widespread custom of wassailing the apple orchards, which took place around Christmas, at the New Year, or at Twelfth Night. The intention behind the custom was to frighten away evil spirits (which dislike noise) and to encourage the trees to bear a good crop. Cider and toast or cake were taken into the orchard at night, and the cider was poured round the roots of the oldest or the best tree. The toast or cake soaked in cider was placed in a fork of the tree and the tree was itself toasted in cider. A song was sung to it at this stage in the proceedings,

Wassailing an apple orchard at Dunster, Somerset.

the words varying from one district to another. The apple trees at Upton St Leonard's near Painswick in Gloucestershire were serenaded with

> Blowe, blowe, bear well,
> Spring well in April,
> Every sprig and every spray
> Bear a bushel of apples against
> Next new year's day.[17]

Finally, shotguns were fired into the branches, or noises made with trays and pans, cow-horns or the human voice, to frighten away the evil spirits and to wake up the trees.[18]

Once the rituals necessary for promoting crop growth had been duly performed, the people eagerly awaited the fruition of their crops, and prepared for the important harvest celebrations. These incorporated a number of ancient fertility rituals. Before we describe them, however, we must not forget other, living, 'crops' which were equally important to their producers. We are thinking of the herdsmen tending their animals, and the fishermen casting their nets at sea.

On 1 May shepherds and other herdsmen in the Scottish Highlands would perform a ritual designed to protect their animals for the coming year. The procedure was described in the eighteenth century by traveller Thomas Pennant.

On the 1st of May, the herdsmen of every village hold their Bel-tein – a rural sacrifice. They cut out a square trench on the ground, leaving the turf in the middle; on that they make a fire of wood, on which they dress a large caudle of eggs, butter, oatmeal and milk; and bring besides the ingredients of the caudle, plenty of beer and whisky for each of the company must contribute something. The rites begin with spilling some of the caudle on the ground, by way of libation; on that, everyone takes a cake of oatmeal upon which are raised nine square knobs, each dedicated to some particular being, the supposed preserver of their flocks and herds, or to some particular animal, the real destroyer of them; each person then turns his face to the fire, breaks off a knob, and flinging it over his shoulder says 'This I give to thee, *preserve thou my horses*; this to thee, *preserve thou my sheep*' and so on. After that they use the same ceremony to the noxious animals. 'This I give to thee, O Fox! Spare thou my lambs; this to thee O Hooded Crow, this to thee O Eagle.' When the ceremony is over they dine on the caudle; and after the feast is finished, what is left is hid by two persons deputed for that purpose; but on the next Sunday they re-assemble and finish the reliques of the first entertainment.[19]

Fishermen's ceremonies aimed at producing a good catch have largely been absorbed by Christian blessing ceremonies, as at Rogationtide mentioned earlier, but at Worle in Avon it was the fishermen's practice to put a white stone on a certain cairn and say

> Ina pic winna,
> Send me a good dinner.[20]

Today fishing is a dying industry in Britain, and blessing ceremonies are likewise few, though at one time many fisheries were blessed at the start of the fishing season. At Abbotsbury in Dorset, Garland Day is held on Old May Day (13 May), and originally marked the opening of the fishing season there. The seamen's children made flower garlands which were placed in the fishing boats, and later, after a church service and when the boats set sail, the garlands were thrown in the sea to bring good fishing. Now that there is no longer a fishing fleet at Abbotsbury, garlands are still made, but they are carried round the village. Some years, one is thrown into the sea as a tribute to its importance to Abbotsbury in the past.[21]

Abbotsbury Garland Day. This photograph was taken at a time when the garlands were still carried out to sea in boats.

As the agricultural year progressed, the culmination of the year's labours grew nearer – harvest time. The importance of this time is shown by the widespread nature of harvest customs and rituals, and their vitality. Most of them only died out when machinery took over the harvest, and even now traces still remain.[22] Originally, the start of harvest was an important time. It was celebrated at the Celtic Lughnasad (usually 1 August), and although customs marking the start (as opposed to the completion) of harvesting are not widely recorded, folklore collector Alexander Carmichael noted what took place in the Highlands and islands of Scotland.

The day the people began to reap the corn was a day of commotion and ceremonial in the townland. The whole family repaired to the field dressed in their best attire to hail the God of the harvest. Laying his bonnet on the ground, the father of the family took up his sickle, and facing the sun, he cut a handful of corn. Putting the handful of corn three times sunwise round his head, the man raised the 'Iolach Buana' reaping salutation. The whole family took up the strain and praised the God of the harvest, who gave them corn and bread, food and flocks, wool and clothing, health and strength, and peace and plenty.[23]

Carmichael also recorded incantations with pagan overtones which would have been chanted at the time of beginning the harvest.[24]

The Christian festival celebrated on 1 August was Lammas (originally Lughnasad), when (or on the nearest Sunday) new corn was taken into the church and offered as the first harvest thanksgiving.[25] On the Isle of Man Lammas Day was celebrated by climbing mountains and visiting wells. There is evidence, from a description of the mountaintop antics as rude and indecent behaviour, that the day may have had some fertility significance. The Church disapproved of the earthy revels, and the custom was emasculated, becoming a Sunday outing into the hills 'to gather blaeberries'.[26]

A traditional game once played in Wales at harvest time also has overtones of a fertility ritual. Called *Rhibo*, it was played by the men and women who had gathered at the farm to cut the wheat. Six men stood in two rows of three each, holding the hands of the man opposite. Across their arms lay a man and a woman side by side, who were then thrown up into the air several times.[27]

Harvest was a joyful time, as the surviving folklore shows, but with undertones of menace. It was not all celebration, and the correct procedures must be followed in order to guarantee the success of the following year's harvest. The cutting of the last sheaf or 'neck' was a critical point, and the form taken by this ceremony varied from one

Cutting the corn with a sickle in the fourteenth century, an illustration from the Luttrell Psalter (top). Compare it with the photograph of harvesting corn with a sickle at Lammington in Lanarkshire (Strathclyde), Scotland, at the beginning of this century, and see how little the method changed over 600 years.

district to another. The 'neck' (a Norse word meaning 'sheaf') was the last remaining group of corn stalks, embodying the spirit of the corn, and no one wanted to deal the final cut and 'kill' it. So all the reapers stood at a distance and threw their sickles in turn, until the neck was finally cut, the responsibility then being a joint one. In some places, however, the successful reaper was fêted, and in Herefordshire he sat opposite the master at the harvest supper table.[28] Also, in some areas the neck took the form of an animal: in Herefordshire a mare, in Galloway a hare. The corn was tied to resemble the animal in question. Sir J. G. Frazer noted many other animal embodiments elsewhere in Europe, such as the wolf, dog, cock, cat, goat, bull, cow, ox, pig, and many others. He saw this as indicating 'the sacramental character of the harvest-supper', in that the slain animal would then be eaten by the harvesters.[29]

Elsewhere the last sheaf was personified and was known either as the Corn Dolly, or Kern Baby, or some similar name denoting a maiden, or as the Carlin, Old Woman, or Cailleach, denoting a hag. In Glen Lyon (Tayside), if the harvest was good the last sheaf was

Cutting the 'calacht' (last sheaf) at Toome, County Antrim, Northern Ireland, in the early 1900s.

A Kern baby. It was stuck on a pole and held aloft, the people dancing round it and curtseying to it. Then it was taken to the barn, where it presided over the harvest supper. At Whalton in Northumberland, where this Kern baby was made, it was taken to the church for the harvest festival and kept there throughout the next year.

149

dressed like a young girl; if bad, it was dressed like an old woman. The Scottish Cailleach would be thrown into the field of a farmer with his harvest unfinished, and he would pass it on. The last farmer in the sequence would have a Cailleach to support during the winter, and so there was a real incentive to make progress with the harvest![30] In some areas of Britain, the dressed sheaf was ceremonially taken back to the farm with the last load, and later was prominently displayed at the harvest supper. As one of the many variations, in Cambridgeshire the last (or Horkey) load was accompanied by the Lord and his Queen, who sat on the cart which was decorated with branches. The Queen was sometimes a man dressed as a woman (an intriguing aspect of fertility magic which we investigate in Chapter 11), and sometimes she was a girl carrying a bunch of wheat and flowers. Spectators watching the procession would throw buckets of water over the cart, perhaps to encourage the rain needed for next year's crop.[31] In some parts of Wales, such as Pembrokeshire, where the last sheaf was carried home by hand, the women of the farm would collect water in their utensils and try to wet the sheaf. Good luck attended the bearer if he got it home dry, which was often achieved by deception and horseplay.[32] Water sprinkling and its fertility significance are discussed further in Chapter 11.

Just as the corn spirit in animal form was sacrificed when the last sheaf was cut, so may the personified sheaves have represented sacrifices. The folklore of the recent past shows the harvest rituals as shadows of their former selves, carrying mere suggestions of the intensity with which the rituals were originally performed. It has been suggested, though there is no direct evidence, that a living 'Corn Maiden' was sacrificed, or perhaps the sacrifice was the reaper who cut the last sheaf, in order to restore life to the corn spirit and thus ensure the continuance of the agricultural cycle.

The last sheaf or 'neck', whether made into a 'dolly' or not, was usually kept until the following year. It was hung in the farmhouse for good luck in many districts. In the Isle of Man, the 'baban ny mheillea' (doll of the harvest) was the figure of a woman formed from a bunch of ears of corn with straw about 12 inches long, which had been cut from the last sheaf. This stood on the kitchen chimney piece until the next harvest, while the last sheaf itself was kept in the barn for a year.[33] In the Llansilin area of Clwyd, the last sheaf was sometimes placed in the stackyard in the fork of a tree, and also in the same area corn from the last sheaf was sometimes mixed with the seed corn at the

Carrying home the last load, with the last sheaf being held aloft.

next sowing, 'so as to teach it to grow'.[34] Sometimes the last sheaf was ploughed back into the soil when ploughing started the next year,[35] or it was the dolly made from the last sheaf that was ploughed in.[36] In upland parts of Somerset, the last stook was left standing in the field to rot away.[37] In parts of Devon the last sheaf was burnt after the *next* harvest,[38] or sometimes given to the best beast after being hung over the kitchen table for a year.[39] This also happened in the Scottish Highlands, where the sheaf went to the horses at the start of ploughing, or to a pregnant mare or cow, or to the poultry.[40] These examples show that the last sheaf usually ensured the continuance of some aspect of farming, thereby demonstrating the fertilizing power of the corn spirit which was embodied within it.

As well as corn dollies being made from the straw of the last sheaf, to hang in the farmhouse, stack decorations were also made in some places.[41] Today, all we have is corn dollies to remind us of the varied and vital rituals of harvest-time. The making of corn dollies is now a widespread craft, and they can be seen for sale in most country craft shops. There are many intricate designs, varying from one district to another, such as the Cambridgeshire bell, the Suffolk horseshoe and

The 'neck' is hung up for the harvest supper in the barn at the farm of Tremough Barton, Mabe, Cornwall.

'The little cage', a corn dolly from Yockleton, Shropshire, made in 1928 by an 84-year-old farm worker who took one each year to his employer's house 'for luck'.

whip, the Norfolk lantern, the Durham chandelier, the Vale of Pickering chalice, the Kent ivy girl, the Staffordshire knot, and Northamptonshire horns.[42] Although it is good that the art has not died, the dollies of the 1980s are lifeless objects when compared with the living embodiments of the corn spirit which preceded them.

Corn dollies of wheat, oats and barley straw from Llangynllo, Powys.

Echoes of the old customs, which died out with mechanization, remained in isolated districts where the harvest was still done by hand. Naomi Mitchison wrote of a 'harvest experience' in 1937 on the island of Vallay off North Uist in the Western Isles. She was helping two old men who were gathering their barley crop, when

The two old men came up to me and I became aware that something was happening though I did not at once see what, nor did I realize that it was I who had bound the last sheaf in the field. The two of them put a straw twist round my waist, knotting it as though I too had been a sheaf. They spoke slowly and seriously in Gaelic and I do not know what they said but at the end one of them spoke in English saying to me: 'go back to the house and keep the binding and you will get your wish'. It seems to me now that I was clearly the cailleach, the

A corner of Blythburgh church, Suffolk, decorated for the harvest festival in 1977.

old woman (or maiden), the sacrifice. At the time I felt rather shaken and I did not as a matter of fact get my wish. Perhaps I took the binding off too soon.[43]

Even after the combine-harvester turned the harvest into a mechanical exercise, sometimes a kind of race-memory broke through, as Celia Gardner here describes.

From a field path in Hertfordshire I was watching a combine-harvester gather up the corn. Back and forth it went, leaving paths of straw in its wake. Almost at the end of the last strip of standing corn the young farmer stopped his machine, leapt from the seat and knelt on the ground. Taking a handful of growing corn, he knotted it into a crude 'doll', then climbed back into his seat and drove off.[44]

Harvest suppers still survive in country districts, though without the corn dolly in pride of place. Ironically the strongest 'survivor' today is the Church's harvest festival, a custom which only started in 1843 when the Reverend R. S. Hawker of Morwenstow in Cornwall revived the Lammas celebration but changed the time to after the harvest rather than before it.[45] The church becomes a living building when decorated with sheaves of corn, loaves of bread, freshly gathered vegetables, fruit and flowers, and the enthusiasm with which this festival is celebrated indicates that, with the dying out of the old harvest customs, people still feel a need to mark and give thanks for the annual fruition of the crops. In some churches the pagan corn dolly can even be seen on display, to remind us how the corn spirit used to preside over the ritual of harvest.

9 The ritual sacrifice of the divine victim

'In the ritual shedding of blood it is not the taking of life but the giving of life that really is fundamental, for blood is not death but life.'

E. O. James, *Origins of Sacrifice*[1]

Among primitive societies in many parts of the world it was the custom to kill their kings either as soon as they showed the slightest sign of old age or whilst they still reigned with full health and vigour.[2] The positions both of chief or king and tribal medicine man or magician would often devolve upon one individual who was expected to regulate the natural forces so that the kingdom would prosper, the hunting be successful, the land be fertile and the people flourish.[3] In more complex societies with a hereditary monarchy and a more evolved theology, the king was seen not only as a man but also as the god incarnate. Frazer tells us that

The belief that kings possess magical or supernatural powers by virtue of which they can fertilize the earth and confer other benefits on their subjects would seem to have been shared by the ancestors of all the Aryan races from India to Ireland, and it has left clear traces of itself in our own country down to modern times.[4]

It is these clear traces of this belief in the divine power of the British kings that this chapter intends to explore.

Initially, it might seem illogical that the god/king should be killed at the height of his powers when all was well in the kingdom, but the ever-present possibility of rapid physical, moral and spiritual decline throughout the land should an enfeebled monarch cling to power was such that all, including the god/king himself, recognized the intrinsic wisdom of the customary course of action. With the death of the king the sacred spirit was freed to incorporate with his successor and thus the continued flow of psychic energy was ensured.[5] The ritual death also became a blood sacrifice. Blood was thought to contain the essence of the life force, and by the outpouring of the divine victim's life-essence, preferably directly on to the soil, the union of heaven and earth was perpetuated and the vital energies were renewed throughout the land.[6]

On a more prosaic level the repeated sacrifice of the king as the divine victim would present those governed with the necessity of frequently finding a new head of state who would exhibit the virtues of his predecessor. There was also the problem of the victim himself, who, at the height of his vigour, virility and popularity, might prefer to seek some other way of perpetuating his people's well-being. Thus the concept of the substitute victim evolved. In Britain he was usually of royal blood or closely connected to the king by marriage, or else a member of the Christian clergy. Whichever line he came from he was promoted to great position within the land until he often wielded more power than the king himself. During this time he received the full protection of the king until the appointed date of sacrifice arrived. This usually revolved around the number seven, and on a multiple of seven years, either in the reign or the age of the king, the divine victim was sacrificed without mercy. Esoterically the number seven represents the blending of the heavenly three with the earthly four, and so contains both spiritual and temporal energies. It symbolizes the completion of a cycle resulting in perfect order.[7] The sacrifice usually took place on one of the four great festivals of the pre-Christian religion and would therefore occur in February, May, August or November. The divine victim was buried with full honours and his body was often dismembered and distributed to various centres throughout the land and there buried. This practice stemmed from the belief that the corpse still contained fertilizing and life-giving energies which were thereby broadcast more effectively. In Scotland and France the divine victim sometimes met his death by fire and then the ashes were scattered over the land.[8]

Academically, little is known or understood of these beliefs or rituals as performed in Britain. In pre-Christian times few written records were kept and those which may have been found by the first Christian missionaries were usually destroyed as being pagan and therefore of the Devil. The writings which have survived from these early centuries come from the pens of monks and could not reflect an accurate view of the life and practices of the indigenous peoples. Dr Margaret Murray (1863–1963, Egyptologist and folklorist) was the major English academic who researched this area of history and her books provide a wealth of evidence which shows that the pre-Christian religion, which she refers to as the 'Old Religion' or the 'Dianic Cult', survived in remote parts of the countryside until the period of the Commonwealth.[9] Dr Murray's theories have met with much academic opposition, as innovative thought so often does, and though in her enthusiasm she sometimes overstated her case, when viewed in the widest context such as this book is attempting, there is little doubt that her thesis has great validity. She has traced sacrifices of divine victims from Saxon times to the Stuarts, when the practice finally stopped, and readers who wish to delve into the detail of this subject are referred to her two books *The Divine King in England* and *The God of the Witches*.[10] Here we shall briefly outline the careers and fates of three of the more famous characters who were destined to be divine victims, though Margaret Murray has identified a number of others.[11]

William Rufus was the third son of William the Conqueror who, with his Norman barons, had successfully invaded and overrun England in 1066. In 1087 the Conqueror died and William Rufus became King William II. It should be appreciated that at this time the Christian Church was not the dominant, all-pervasive force that it later became. It was in effect a strange religion that had been introduced from abroad some 500 years earlier. Although it had been nominally adopted by most of the rulers at whom the early Christian missionaries had logically directed their efforts, it had hardly touched the deep-rooted beliefs and practices of the common people. There was no atmosphere of instant mass conversion and they continued to worship their own ancient gods, who were naturally labelled 'devils' by the Christian chroniclers. For many centuries some of the kings, nobles and clergy successfully managed to combine both old and new religions. While publicly appearing as devout Christians they continued quietly to observe the practices of the ancient order, known only to one another within their group or 'coven'.

The confidence of William Rufus in himself and his position was such that he openly proclaimed himself to be a pagan and missed few opportunities to deride the Christians or to avail himself of the Church's wealth when he wished. His forebears were pagans and upon becoming king he naturally would consider himself to be both king and the incarnation of God for his people. It is not known why the Latin 'Rufus' (red) was attached to his name. Perhaps it was because of the colour of his complexion or hair. But red was also the symbolic colour of vitality, life and fertility and would therefore be a symbol of the old pagan religion and of its god/king. As the Devil incarnate of the Christian chroniclers, William Rufus was vilified, but even his enemies had to admit that he displayed the virtues expected of and hoped for in a monarch. He was a good son, an efficient and able ruler, a warm friend, courageous and open-handed. He never broke his word and was generous to his enemies, but ruthless with evildoers.

King William II (William Rufus).

The death of William Rufus occurred on the significant date of 2 August 1100, as would befit a divine victim. It was referred to in the records as 'the morrow of Lammas', Lammas being 1 August and the last of the four annual festivals of the pagan year. He was crowned in 1087 and on the first seven-year anniversary of his reign in 1094 his archbishop Anselm was charged with high treason but fled to safety before sentence could be carried out. Archbishops or chancellors have more than once been placed in the position of substitute for the divine sacrifice, but evidently not always willingly. The next year in which a sacrificial victim could be expected was 1101, but William Rufus was killed in 1100. Why should this be? Although his exact birthdate is not known, it was probably in 1057 or 1058, which would give him the significant age of forty-two (being six periods of seven years). This, falling on the turn of the century, would be a concurrence of overwhelming significance, and at such a time no substitute would suffice but the god/king himself must die.

The sacrifice of William Rufus was carefully planned with his co-operation to take place on a hunting trip in the New Forest, Hampshire. The accounts we have say that he could not sleep the night before and called for lights to be brought so that he could talk with his companions. In the morning he made his final arrangements, to ensure a continuity of rule after his death, and then ate and drank well at midday. While he was dressing for the hunt, six new arrows were brought to him and he gave two to Walter Tyrrel, remarking, 'It is right that the sharpest arrows should be given to him who knows how to deal deadly strokes with them.' He is also recorded as later saying to Tyrrel, 'Walter, do thou justice according to those things which thou hast heard', to which Tyrrel replied: 'So I will, my lord.' It is hardly conceivable that the sacrifice of the god/king at the turn of the century would take place without an appropriate ritual being enacted, and though this would be unknown and unrecorded by the chroniclers, we believe it likely that this ceremony occurred either in the early hours of the morning or, perhaps more likely, during the afternoon, in the sunlit forest as would befit a pagan god of fertility, and immediately before the sacrificial act itself.

The accounts of how William Rufus met his death differ in detail but it is said that the hunt continued until late in the day. William Rufus shot at a stag which he slightly wounded. He watched it disappear into the distance, shielding his eyes from the setting sun. Tyrrel then shot at another animal but his arrow glanced off the hide,

The New Forest, Hampshire, close to the spot where William Rufus died. The exact spot is marked by an unattractive pillar known as the Rufus Stone.

or the antlers, or he missed and the arrow glanced off a tree and struck the King, who without a word broke off the end of the arrow and fell upon the projecting shaft to die quickly. Another version says that the King's bowstring broke as he shot at the stag and he called out to Tyrrel to shoot. When Tyrrel hesitated, William Rufus ordered him to 'Draw, draw your bow for the Devil's sake and let fly your arrow, or it will be the worse for you.' (It has been pointed out that the word 'Devil' was used by the recording Christians for any non-Christian deity, and that he would in fact have used a deity's name in his exclamation and not the word 'Devil'.) Here too it is said that he hastened his death with cool deliberation by falling on to the projecting shaft. In either event, his blood spilled on to the English soil and due ritual had been observed. William Rufus's body was left to lie until recovered by Purkis, a charcoal burner, who placed it on his cart and drove to Winchester by way of Otterbourne, where today King's Lane and King's Mead record the route and a resting place on the final journey. Tyrrel returned to his own country of Normandy unpursued and lived there without hindrance. Within a few hours the expected news of the King's death was known in many parts of the kingdom.

This is the esoteric view of the death of William Rufus, first expounded by Margaret Murray and subsequently supported by knowledge of such pagan practices as we set out in this book. Needless to say, it is not the view of conventional historians who know nothing of the esoteric pagan practices and see historical events and people solely in terms of power politics.[12]

Thomas à Becket, who was sacrificed in 1170 within the precincts of Canterbury Cathedral in Kent, was at that time Archbishop of Canterbury, and he is a major example of the divine substitute being an ecclesiastic. Margaret Murray has remarked on the strange, undetermined relationship between English kings and their arch-bishops of Canterbury, whom she equates with the Arch-Flamen (i.e. pagan high priest). In his early years Becket was a soldier and diplomat. In 1155 the young Henry II made him Chancellor and they were obviously the greatest of friends and companions. In 1162 the King insisted that the reluctant Becket should become Archbishop of Canterbury, but Becket, once installed, soon began to fall out with the King over political matters affecting the Church and State. He fled to France in 1164, returning six years later. But his quarrel with the King was soon renewed, and Henry, then in Normandy, issued orders

THOMAS BECKET
ARCHBISHOP * SAINT * MARTYR
DIED HERE
TUESDAY 29TH - DECEMBER
1170

The site of Becket's murder in Canterbury Cathedral.

which resulted in four knights hurrying to Canterbury. The records show that on the afternoon of 29 December 1170 Becket met and talked with the four knights, assuring them that he would not flee. But later his monks who knew the coming danger but probably not the esoteric reasoning behind it manhandled him against his wishes into the refuge of the cathedral. He kept away from the High Altar and went into the north transept. At the appointed hour of sunset the knights entered from the cloisters and Becket commended himself to 'the doom of God, St Mary and to blessed Dionysius'. Then he stretched his neck forward and the knights killed him with their swords. The final words of the drama were spoken by the knights who said, 'He wished to be king, he wished to be more than king, just let him be king.' As with William Rufus, Becket's death was known of in many parts of Britain within a few hours. Soon after his death miracles were being ascribed to Becket's influence and chroniclers such as William of Canterbury, an eye-witness, wrote detailed analyses of his death, drawing parallels between the incident and the death of the supreme divine victim, Christ. The King did penance for the murder by undergoing flagellation, this being interpreted by Margaret Murray as a ritual drawing of the monarch's blood upon the death of his substitute. Although popular legend tells that the knights all met with terrible deaths, there are no records that show this, and at least one became wealthy and died undramatically fourteen years later.[13]

The story of Joan of Arc, our third divine victim, has been told many times and will only be dealt with briefly here. She was a French peasant girl born in 1412 who in 1428 became convinced that she had a mission to save France from the English. She eventually gained an audience with the Dauphin and convinced him by a secret 'sign' to take her claims seriously. She asked for armed men to command and said that her Lord, the 'King of Heaven', had sent her to drive the English back and to lead the Dauphin to Reims, to be crowned King of France. The troops followed her with fervour and devotion, and she succeeded in making the Dauphin King of France, Charles VII. But the English were still occupying parts of France and in a skirmish in 1430 Joan was captured by the Burgundians and sold to the English, who tried her for heresy and witchcraft, and she was eventually burnt at the stake.[14]

The idea of an eighteen-year-old peasant girl leading an army to victory defies normal explanations. But within her story there are certain points which if viewed in the light of our thesis of the divine victim indicate that Joan may have been acting out this ritual as she released France from the English occupiers. Her birthplace of Domrémy was known to be a stronghold of pagan belief and practice and her first contact with the 'voices' which guided her occurred at a fairy tree near her home, a clear indication of pagan tree veneration. Also, before the Dauphin would accept her cause he arranged that she should be closely questioned by Churchmen to ensure that her mission and motives were compatible with Christianity. When asked

An official copy of Joan of Arc's trial, with a drawing of Joan in the margin.

to select a protector in battle she chose Gilles de Rais, an aristocratic soldier who was probably also of the old religion. Nine years later he was brought before an ecclesiastical court and charged with heresy. He confessed to numerous crimes and was hung. Here was another inexplicable death which Margaret Murray suggests was that of a divine victim.

Joan herself knew that her time would be of short duration and at one time she told the Dauphin to 'Make the most of me, for I shall last only one year.'[15] When Joan was captured by the Burgundians she languished in their prison for six months. It could have been expected that her wealthy friends and the French King would have released her with a ransom, and yet there is no record of any such offer nor any attempt at rescue, and so the Burgundians made the best deal they could and sold her to their allies the English, at whose hands she met her death. During her trial she never used the commonly accepted terms of 'Our Lord', 'Our Saviour' or 'Christ' but always referred to 'My Lord' or 'the King of Heaven' or simply 'God', and finally during her imprisonment and trial after a period of self-doubt and recantation she seems to have resolved to meet her fate and so resumed the wearing of men's clothing. Great stress is laid on this in the records, and it could be seen as a symbol of her resumption of the position of the God Incarnate. A parallel in the traditional customs is the dressing of a man in women's clothes, the she-male figure, which will be discussed at the end of Chapter 11. This interpretation of Joan's action seems to have been implicitly understood by both her judges and the people at large.

Some of the traditional customs still practised in Britain (or fairly recently abandoned) appear to include traces of the ritual sacrifice of the divine victim. We have already discussed in the last chapter the possible sacrifice of the Corn Maiden at harvest-time, and in Chapter 10 we shall describe mummers' plays which have a clear theme of death and resurrection in the killing of St George and his magical revival. Sword dances were originally also part of mummers' plays, and they too contain a ritual killing. These dances came into Britain from Scandinavia and they still flourish in parts of northern England. The significant moment in the sword dance is when the blades are woven together in a star shape which is called a 'lock' or 'glass', and this is sometimes placed symbolically around the neck of the sacrificial victim who is often the 'fool' of the group. At Grenoside (near Sheffield, South Yorkshire), the lock is placed around the neck of the leader who wears a fox-pelt hat with the animal's head in front, and this hat is 'decapitated' at the appropriate time in the performance.[16] The fool is also the sacrificial victim in the Haxey Hood Game, already described in Chapter 7. Before the game starts he mounts a stone in front of the church to make his welcoming speech, and as he does so a pile of damp straw is lit at his feet. Originally this 'Smoking the Fool' custom took place the day after the Haxey Hood Game and the fool was suspended from a tree and swung backwards and forwards through the smoke from a fire below, finally being allowed to fall into the smouldering straw. This hazardous custom was replaced by the present practice, but there remain clear indications of a ritual sacrifice by fire, which probably originally took place on the mid-winter solstice.[17]

The springtime customs which until recently were widely practised with great energy and enthusiasm on Binding Monday and Tuesday at Hocktide (the Monday and Tuesday after Low Sunday) also suggest that the original purpose was the capture of a sacrificial victim. The idea was for men to capture women and hold them to ransom, and for the women to do the same with the men. 'Binding' refers to the practice of using ropes to bind the victims, only setting them free when a forfeit was paid. The men would be the victims on one of the

The Grenoside sword dancers demonstrate the 'death' of their leader.

'Smoking the Fool' at Haxey.

days, the women on the other. Today Hocktide is only celebrated at Hungerford in Berkshire, and with ceremonies somewhat different from the earlier practices just described. 'Tutti-men' carrying decorated poles are entitled to stop any woman in the street and demand a kiss, in return for which an orange is given from the top of the tutti-pole. An historical explanation for Hocktide suggested that the ceremonies commemorated the victory over the Danes in 1002, but this was undoubtedly a late attempt to explain a custom whose pagan origins are lost in distant antiquity.[18]

The chalking of a human figure on the Yule log (see Chapter 10) before it was burnt was possibly a remnant of human sacrifice at the mid-winter solstice. The burning of effigies of witches during the last century, particularly in Scotland, may also have stemmed from a practice which originally provided both a sacrificial victim and a means of destroying evil powers. When Queen Victoria was at Balmoral, she was vastly entertained at Hallowe'en when a huge fire was built opposite the main entrance to the house. A procession of kilted clansmen and skirling pipers marched to the fire and in their midst was a trolley carrying the effigy of the 'Shandy dann', a hideous

This 1925 photograph shows the Tutti-men of Hungerford demanding kisses from bashful nurses.

old crone or witch. After an indictment of her crimes and evil ways had been read out, she was hurled into the roaring fire amid general rejoicing.[19]

The concept of the scapegoat who bears away the sins and evils of a community has great affinity with the divine victim, and a custom called 'Riding the Lord' which was practised until the mid-nineteenth century at Neston in Cheshire appears to embody this idea. Here on Easter Monday a man would ride a donkey through the village while the populace pelted him with garbage of every description. Afterwards he was paid for his trouble and went on his way. The origin of this custom is unknown, and the only explanation for it was that it 'had always been done'. Rather similar was 'Riding the Black Lad' which was practised until the 1930s on Easter Monday at Ashton under Lyne in Greater Manchester. The effigy of a knight in black armour and cloak was mounted on a horse and paraded through the town accompanied by a group of retainers and musicians. Finally he was taken down and destroyed with stones and bullets. Although there is a local tradition which identifies the Black Lad with Sir Ralph de Assheton, a harsh landlord of the fifteenth century, and the ceremony

The Burryman at South Queensferry.

as celebrating his eventual downfall, there is no evidence to support this and folklorists consider this explanation unlikely.[20] But there remain the clear indications of a ritual sacrifice which doubtless took place in the centuries when a living victim, not an effigy, took his last ride.

The ancient figure of the Burryman in the fishing ports of eastern Scotland may also have been a scapegoat originally. He was paraded around the town, his clothing covered with burrs and red herrings suspended by their tails from the brim of his hat. In 1864 hundreds of people in Fraserburgh took part in the parade, by which it was hoped to change the luck of the fishing, but they were not successful and the custom lapsed.[21] One Burryman remains today and he parades on the second Friday in August at South Queensferry on the Firth of Forth (Lothian). He is completely covered from head to foot in burrs and they cover his face too. His hat is covered in roses and he holds a flower-covered staff in each hand. The Burryman spends the day touring the town while his assistants collect money from well-wishers, and at the end of the day the collection is counted and divided among them. The Burryman's role of scapegoat seems in recent centuries to have been converted to that of the bringer of fertility, but conceivably the strange custom of covering him in burrs could have stemmed from a time when, as scapegoat, burrs were thrown at him by the populace, these symbolizing all the evils of which the people wished to rid themselves. They stuck to him and were then carried away. The Burryman himself might originally have finished the day as a sacrificial victim.[22]

Today it is difficult to understand how ritual sacrifice could have been condoned, but it is evident[23] that at one time throughout the world there was a generally held belief that sacrifice was essential if the well-being of the land and its peoples were to be secured. Their concern with fertility overruled all other considerations.

10 Traditional customs with fertility overtones: banishing winter and welcoming spring

'In celebrating the festivals and through seeking the ancient sites of the standing stones, holy wells, etc., we can reconnect with the living forces of the Earth, and come to feel once again the Earth planet as a living being, revealed as the Earth Goddess.'

Adam McLean, *The Four Fire Festivals*[1]

The many traditional customs of which we write in this book are but the degenerate remnants of rituals of an earlier age when the energies of the people were fiercely directed towards the continuance of fertility. They instinctively understood that the fertility of the Earth Mother was essential for their own well-being and for the health and vitality of their crops and cattle, and to this end the cyclic, seasonal round of birth, growth, fruition and death was punctuated by the appropriate rituals and festivals. In more recent centuries there was a lingering sense of the basic necessity of continuing these customs as they gradually fell into disuse in all but the most remote areas of the country, but today the overwhelming triumph of urbanization has reduced most of these hitherto vital practices to a few nostalgic customs. Despite this, the re-enactment of obscure rituals still has its instinctive attraction for many people.

The Celts understood that the seasonal cycle must start with the onset of the cold and darkness of winter which will presently be challenged by the ever-strengthening rays of the emerging sun, and so the start of the Celtic year was marked by the festival of Samhain when fires were lit on the sacred hills at dusk on 31 October, latterly known as Hallowe'en. This was a time when spirits were abroad and the events of the coming year could be foreseen. Up to the end of the last century in the remoter areas of Wales and Scotland, marked stones were cast into the fire, and their condition when they were retrieved the following morning indicated the individual's fortune for the coming year.[2] It was also customary to put out the house fires and relight them from the ceremonial fire which had been kindled by friction.[3] In many places youths jumped through the flames and smoke, and later the ashes were scattered over the fields or a blazing torch was carried round the boundaries in an act of saining (blessing and protecting).[4] Although of serious intent, these ceremonies were enacted in a spirit of joy. Potatoes and apples were roasted on the fire, and the people sang and danced around it.[5] The follies and miseries of the past season were consumed in the purging flames and a new year was ahead of them. In Wales when the embers burnt low the cry was given: 'May the tailless Black Sow take the hindmost', and the assembled company raced away downhill to the safety of their homes.[6] Often an effigy which in recent centuries was called the 'witch' or 'hag' was burned on the fire. This did not represent any human witch but more likely symbolized all the malevolent forces with which the community had had to contend in the preceding year.[7] Today all that is left of this festival are the bonfires on 5 November and the political bogeyman of Guy Fawkes which has replaced the traditional effigy.[8]

The winter solstice is on 22 December, the shortest day of the year, when the sun rises and sets at its most southerly point. After this the hours of daylight gradually lengthen as the seasons continue their progress towards spring and summer. This was an important point in the annual cycle and was once again marked by a fire ceremony. Due to the rigours of the winter weather, this ceremony was celebrated inside the house. Its high point was the bringing in of the Yule log (or block or clog) and its ceremonial burning on the principal hearth.

The Yule log.

Traditionally the log was never paid for, but always came from the householder's own tree or was a gift from a neighbour. It was dragged back to the house by horses or oxen after being decorated with evergreens, and sometimes had ale or cider poured over it and was sprinkled with corn before being lit. It could only be lit with a piece from the previous year's log and was then kept smouldering, sometimes for as long as twelve days, until the time came for it to be ceremonially quenched. The Yule log would have to be a large block of wood, and was usually of oak, ash or beech. In some dwellings it was laid in a pit below the hearth with the usual house fire burning on top. By this means the block was not rapidly consumed and so there were always some remnants left. These were saved to protect the house during the year ahead from lightning or fire. If steeped in water which was then drunk by cows, it would help them in calving, and the ashes when scattered on the fields prevented mildew on the crops. The part of the Yule log which had not been charred was prized by ploughmen who used it for the wedge on their plough, thereby bringing its fertilizing influences close to the receptive earth. A West Country variation of the Yule log was the ash faggot which was a bundle of ash sticks bound together with ash or withy bands. As the flames burst the bands, toasts of cider or ale were drunk and the young unmarried women, each of whom had chosen a band of their own, could foretell who would be first to marry.

Evidently the Yule log was expected to perpetuate the well-being of the homestead and the fertility of its lands and beasts, but at the same time as the vital fertilizing powers were invoked, the powers of evil and death were repulsed. In the Scottish Highlands the head of the house would first carve the log into a semblance of an old woman, known as Cailleach Nollaich, or Christmas Old Wife. This was ceremonially brought home and placed on the peat fire until completely consumed, while the assembled family drank toasts to the triumph over evil. In Cornwall a figure of a man was sometimes chalked on to the Yule log, to fade slowly into the smouldering wood, and this probably had the same intent as the Scottish practice.[9]

At this winter solstice fire festival a reaffirmation of the ever-present vitality of the vegetation was made by decorating the interior of the house with evergreens. Holly, ivy and mistletoe were, and are, traditionally used (though any green midwinter leaves were suitable), and a sprig of holly was kept throughout the year to protect the house and occupants from fire and lightning. Whereas the Samhain fires of 1

November were of Celtic origin, the Winter Solstice fires stemmed from our Scandinavian and Saxon connections and were most avidly perpetuated in those areas of Britain where their influence had been strongest. With the advent of Christianity the midwinter festival, which was practised over a wide area of Europe, was designated as Christ's birthdate, and during the ensuing centuries the pagan fertility practices became overlaid with Christian symbolism.

It was at this same season that the Mummers acted out their symbolic performances, and there are still a few villages in England where the tradition is continued. At specific outdoor sites and private houses and pubs the short ritual of death and regeneration is enacted, usually on Christmas Eve or Boxing Day. The principal characters in these 'rustic' entertainments are usually St George (as we shall see later, the figure of St George is associated with the Green Man, Jack in the Green, and the May King), the dragon or Turkish knight, and the Doctor. St George fights with the dragon or Turkish knight, receives a fatal wound, and at the point of death is restored to full vigour by the Doctor who administers his magic medicine. Other characters who

Decorating the home with evergreens at Christmastime.

The Marshfield (Avon) Mummers or 'Paper Boys' (above) perform their play on Boxing Day each year. The photograph, taken in 1966, shows the death. The names of the characters are Father Christmas, Little Man John, King William, Dr Phoenix, Saucy Jack, Tenpenny Nit and Beelzebub.
The Midgley pace-egg play (below).

may appear are Father Christmas, Little John, Robin Hood and Beelzebub, and there are other local variants with characters whose comments in doggerel verse on local affairs are calculated to amuse the audience. In this form the Mumming plays go back to the fifteenth century, but folklorists have no doubt that the original inspiration for the ritual of death and regeneration stretches far beyond this to the pre-Christian era.[10]

Easter celebrates the return of spring and a dominant theme is the giving of Easter eggs. The symbol of the egg is tremendously potent in the human psyche, and is used worldwide. It is more than simply the seed of life, but contains the ideas of rebirth, re-creation and immortality. Throughout Europe eggs have been traditionally used at ploughing and sowing time, sometimes being thrown into the fresh furrows, eaten by the ploughman, or carried by the sowers of the grain.[11] In Shetland, a hen's egg was sometimes placed in the basket of seed corn before sowing, and left there throughout the spring.[12] The egg, being an embodiment of life, was intended to encourage the seed to sprout.

In Britain, Easter egg festivals were once prolific, and some still remain with us. Until the end of the nineteenth century the Mummers would again appear with their Pace-Egg play, which was very much like the Christmas play mentioned above. Known as Pace-Eggers or Jolly-Boys, they would go from house to house with blackened faces and wearing strange costumes, and would give a short performance at each, receiving a gift of decorated Easter eggs or money in return.[13] Sometimes the group would include women who wore men's clothes, while the men were disguised as women. This reversal of the sexual roles is an intriguing aspect of fertility practices which we discuss in the next chapter.[14] One of the last, if not the only, remaining performances of a Pace-Egg play occurs on Good Friday and is performed at Midgley, West Yorkshire, by the pupils of Calder High School. Wearing rosettes and elaborate headgear, they perform outdoors to a fascinated crowd. St George's adversaries are Bold Slasher, Bold Hector, and the Black Prince. The Doctor is there too, as are also the Fool, the King of Egypt, and Tosspot who carries a basket that once would have received eggs but now collects gifts of money.[15]

Pace-egging most often occurred in northern England and is now, as with other traditional customs, continued only by the children. The Pace-Egg plays are largely forgotten and the children simply go from house to house singing or chanting a short begging rhyme:

178

Please, Mrs Whiteleg,
Please to give us an Easter egg.
If you won't give us an Easter egg,
Your hens will lay all addled eggs,
And your cocks lay all stones.[16]

Traditionally the eggs collected by the Pace-Eggers are wrapped in various roots, leaves, flowers or bark which are firmly tied on before the eggs are hardboiled. The vegetable dyes released by boiling imprint colourful patterns on the eggshells and this craft has become a skilled folk-art in some Eastern European countries where it is still practised. In the second half of the nineteenth century these pace-eggs, sometimes covered in gold leaf, could be bought from shops by those who wished to give Easter eggs, but did not want the trouble of

Egg shackling on Shrove Tuesday at Shepton Beauchamp in Somerset.

179

making them. But even then they were gradually being replaced by the mass-produced confectionery eggs that are now sold at Easter.[17]

Having obtained their pace-eggs, the young people would use them in various contests. The simplest was to throw an egg up and catch it, a forfeit being paid for every egg that fell to the ground. In another called egg shackling, two players would each hold a hardboiled egg and take turns in striking their opponent's egg with theirs, the egg which broke first being kept by the winner. In some parts of northern England these sports are still in evidence at Easter, but the southern version of egg shackling, usually played on Shrove Tuesday, seems to have virtually disappeared. Here the unboiled, marked eggs were shaken in a sieve, the last egg to remain uncracked belonging to the winner. Pancakes were made with the cracked eggs.

Another favourite Easter game was egg rolling or trundling, and this still flourishes in some parts of northern England, Scotland and Ireland. A memory of this custom was written by St John Ervine in 1919.

When I was a child I would no more have thought of going out on Easter morning without a real Easter egg than I would have thought of leaving my stocking unsuspended from the foot of my bed on Christmas Eve. A few days before Easter I used to go out to the park, where there were a great many whin bushes, and gather whinblossoms, which I carried home to my mother, who put two eggs in a tin, one for me and one for my sister, and added the whinblossoms and water to them, and set them to boil together until the eggs were hard and the shells were stained a pretty brown hue.

On Easter Monday my sister and I would carry our eggs to a mound in the park called 'The Dummy's Hill', and would trundle them down the slope. All the boys and girls we knew used to trundle their eggs on Easter Monday ... The egg-shell generally cracked during the operation of 'trundling', and then the owner of it solemnly sat down and ate the hardboiled egg, which, of course, tasted very much better than an egg eaten in the ordinary way. 'The Dummy's Hill' was sadly soiled with egg-shells at the end of Easter Monday morning.

My uncle, who was a learned man, said that this custom of 'trundling' eggs was a survival of an old Druidical rite. It seems to me to be queer that we in the North of Ireland should still be practising that ancient ceremony when English children should have completely forgotten it, and should think of an Easter egg, not as a real thing laid by hens and related to the ancient religion of these islands, but as a piece of confectionery turned out by machinery and having no ancient significance whatever.[18]

Until recently, many localities had their traditional slope down which eggs were rolled and then eaten when cracked. At Avenham Park, Preston, Lancashire, crowds of young and old still gather on Easter Monday to roll brightly coloured eggs down the slope to the River Ribble. The tradition is also maintained at Scarborough in North Yorkshire and Barton-upon-Humber in Humberside.[19] It is interesting to note that pace-eggs, or 'peace' or 'paiss' as they are called in Scotland, should really be 'Pasch' eggs, and the name is derived from 'Paschal' which relates to the Jewish Passover.

Some traditional ball games are considered to have a fertility significance and one recorded ritual with such overtones was enacted annually at Easter until the late eighteenth century at Whitchurch, Cardiff. The tennis balls referred to in the following report may originally have been eggs, which would be more appropriate to a fertility rite.

It was usual for every married woman, who had never been blessed with issue, to repair to the church-yard on Easter Monday, being first provided with two dozen tennis balls, one dozen of which were covered with white, and the other dozen with black leather; these were cast by the fair votaress over the church, from the back-ground, and scrambled for by the populace, who assembled for that purpose in front of the building. So imperative was this custom that neither rank nor age were excused, until they were relieved, by the birth of a child, from its annual performance.[20]

Another Easter tradition took place at Chester Cathedral, where as recently as 1839 the Bishop, Dean, and choirboys played a game which involved them in throwing eggs to one another. This happened after Easter morning service, and after their sport they all dined upon gammon and tansy pudding.[21]

The high point of all the spring festivals was undoubtedly May Day, which was usually, though not invariably, held on the first of the month. On this day, throughout Europe, the fertility of the earth was reaffirmed and celebrated. Soon after midnight the young men and women of the community would meet and in the earliest hours before dawn go into the woods. Their purpose was twofold: to cut down and bring home the 'maypole' tree, may blossom, and other greenery; and to practise the emotive and symbolic ritual of orgiastic mating similar to that which took place in the fields at sowing time, already mentioned in Chapter 8.[22] The act of mass union between the sexes in a natural setting has been practised by 'primitive' people in many parts of the world.[23] They instinctively understood a significant truth which modern man is once more beginning to apprehend: that the human mind is inextricably linked to the physical world around it, and is capable of producing and directing tremendous effects on the physical level.[24] By concentrating all their mental and physical energies into an act of procreation they were literally able to cause the natural forces to respond in empathy. As people became more 'civilized', urbanized and increasingly removed from direct interaction with the cosmic life forces, this instinctive knowledge was overlaid and eventually lost.

The May Day festivities were too blatantly orgiastic ever to be assimilated into the ritual of the Christian Church, as had many other pre-Christian practices, and were continually opposed by the clergy. For many years a huge maypole had stood in Cornhill, London, taller than the nearby church which was therefore known as St Andrew Undershaft. In the festivities of 1517 a riot of apprentices had to be quelled by the army[25] and several ringleaders were publicly hanged. The pole was brought down and hung beneath the house eaves along one side of Shaft Alley. In 1662 a fiery sermon was preached from Paul's Cross during which the populace were exhorted to remove this idol from their presence. This was done by each householder sawing up the portion that crossed his property and using it for firewood![26]

Raising the maypole.

As recently as 1583 the Puritan Phillip Stubbes was railing against the still prevalent May celebrations: 'all the yung men and maides, olde men and wives, run gadding over night to the woods, groves, hils, and mountains, where they spend all the night in plesant pastimes; and in the morning they return, bringing with them birch and branches of trees, to deck their assemblies withall.' He then goes on to describe how the decorated maypole ('this stinkyng ydol, rather') is brought home pulled by a team of garlanded oxen, and after being set up, 'then fall they to daunce about it, like as the heathen people did at the dedication of the Idols ... I have heard it credibly reported ... by men of great gravitie and reputation, that of fortie, threescore, or a hundred maides going to the wood over night, there have scaresly the third part of them returned home againe undefiled.'[27]

The Puritans continued to attack the May festivities and succeeded in getting Parliament to ban them in 1644. Orders were issued that all maypoles (which had by then evolved from being freshly hewn trees with loppped branches into permanently erected and decorated poles) should be destroyed by constables or other local officials, who were to be fined five shillings a week (no small sum in those times) until the maypoles were removed.[28] With the restoration of the monarchy in 1660, the maypole once more became a centre of festivities and many were re-erected throughout the land. The return of Charles II was celebrated on 29 May, which became Oak Apple Day, and the celebrations were often combined with those of May Day. On the first May Day after the King's return, a 134-foot-long pole was brought upstream on the Thames to London, and erected in the Strand by twelve sailors. It was gorgeously gilded and decorated and was a focal point for the ensuing celebrations. There it stood until 1717 when it was bought by Sir Isaac Newton to support his new telescope.[29]

Traditionally the young people returning with the maypole would also bring with them greenery and wild flowers from the forest, with which to decorate the house exteriors and the maypole itself. From this evolved such practices as May Birching, where a bough from a certain tree left outside a house conveyed in what esteem the occupants were held. Thus a briar indicated a liar, and a lime, rhyming with prime, was a compliment, as was flowering hawthorn.[30] It was also traditional that mayers should go from house to house announcing the arrival of spring with rhymes, songs and dances which varied in each district and each country across the whole of Europe.[31] In return they were rewarded with gifts of eggs, dried fruit or cake,

Padstow in Cornwall on 1 May, its maypole and the whole village decorated with greenery and flowers.

and, more recently, money. Those who refused to give anything were warned that their crops would fail and their herds would not prosper. As messengers and representatives of the reawakened life force it was the mayers' duty to discourage avarice, which would have a deleterious effect on the well-being of the community, and to encourage mental attitudes of generosity and abundance which would surely be reflected by nature during the coming season. Their actions merited reward because 'the group *sees* spring before anyone else, *brings* it to the village, *shows* it to the others and *hastens* its coming with song, dance and ritual.'[32]

These mayers were led and presided over by the May Queen and King. They were a young couple who were chosen to epitomize the sacred marriage between sky and earth which had been consummated by the many amidst the fields and forests during the earliest hours of that day.[33] It appears that originally the King was chosen by contest, being the winner of a foot-race which finished at the maypole, or the one who could climb to the top of the maypole. At a later time, it was often the May Queen who was chosen by popular consent and who then chose her consort. In Britain today the May King has largely disappeared and the 'crowning' of the May Queen, who is now usually a young girl, is a recent innovation said to have been introduced by the writer John Ruskin in the late nineteenth century when he revived the dying interest in May Day celebrations.[34] As with so many other traditions, May Day has in recent centuries only been maintained by the children. In rural Herefordshire in 1796 a farmer's wife, Anne Hughes, wrote that she made special patties filled with meat, apple, onion, sugar and herbs for the children who called on May Day carrying small garlanded maypoles.[35] But by 1937 the custom had degenerated still further, and folklorist Christina Hole described how in many towns of the north-west

pathetic little bands may be seen in the streets during the last week of April and the first week of May. A little girl in a veil made from an old lace curtain represents the Queen of May, and her attendants usually carry a thin stick with a few ribbons on it. With them goes a boy with a blackened face, whose duty it is generally to collect pennies from the passers-by.[36]

Traditionally May Day was spent in sports and pastimes, eating, drinking and dancing at the foot of the maypole. The dancing was not done with the plaited sashes suspended from the top of the pole that are used today, as this is another custom that was introduced by

Ruskin from southern Europe, where the maypoles were considerably shorter.[37] A few villages in England such as Barwick-in-Elmet, West Yorkshire, and Ickwell Green, Bedfordshire, still retain the traditionally lofty maypole,[38] which is painted with red and white spiral stripes. These colours are often used symbolically in spring festivities, 'red being pre-eminently the colour of life and generative energy',[39] while white indicates a fresh, new beginning. But most May Day ceremonies are now very staid affairs, where children in fancy dress dance around the maypole prettily weaving the coloured sashes, the whole being presided over by the vicar and local school mistress, and with no hint of the original pagan significance.

The May doll or May baby was frequently seen on May morning until the 1930s. A group of young girls would go from house to house with a toy doll dressed in white and placed either in a flower-filled cradle or seated in the centre of a flower garland, made of two hoops intersecting at right angles and covered with ribbons, foliage and flowers. At each stop the children would sing some verses, a typical one being:

Children dancing round a maypole at Aston-on-Clun, Shropshire, part of the Arbor Day celebrations (see Chapter 6) in 1980.

A garland gay we bring you here;
And at your door we stand;
It is a sprout well budded out,
The work of our Lord's hand.[40]

The singers would be rewarded with gifts of food or, latterly, money. The original significance of the children's practice is indicated by this quotation describing the May baby ceremonies that took place in County Louth in Ireland in the early nineteenth century.

On May Day, the figure of a female is made up, fixed upon a short pole and dressed in a fantastic manner, with flowers, ribbons, etc. This figure they call 'The May Baby' ... Around this figure a man and woman (generally his wife) of the humble class, dressed also fantastically with straw, etc., dance to the sound of a fiddle and entertain the people with indecent shows and postures ... These exhibitions cause great merriment among the assembled populace; women who have had no children to their husbands also attend to see this figure and performance, which they imagine will promote fruitfulness in them, and cause them to have children.[41]

On the Isle of Man at the close of the eighteenth century, the Queen of May was not a child but a young woman, chosen from among the daughters of the wealthy farmers. She was attended by twenty maids of honour and also her 'captain' who commanded his troops. These met in mock battle with the troops of the Queen of Winter, who was a man dressed in woman's clothing of furs and woollens. If the Queen of May's troops prevailed all was well, but if the battle went against them and the Queen of May was captured, then she was ransomed, the price being the cost of the day's festivities. The events were concluded by dancing, with a feast in the evening.[42] Similar events took place elsewhere in northern Europe at the springtime festivities, the representative of summer being dressed in leaves, flowers and ivy, and decked in colourful ribbons, while winter wore furs, straw or moss.[43] In the distant past when these ritual struggles originated it was understood that the earth's energies could be stimulated and increased by an expenditure of physical and emotional energy on the part of humanity, so blows, contests and, as shown earlier in this chapter, rough games between the sexes were seen to be the proper means of achieving these ends.[44] The customs just described are but the remnants of earlier fertility rituals.

In Breconshire, a boy was chosen as the King of Summer and another as the King of Winter. Both were hidden completely beneath a covering of birch branches except for their faces, and the summer king wore a brightly beribboned crown while winter wore a crown of holly. Each boy, carried by four men, processed around the village and nearby farms collecting money or beer, and finished at the churchyard where the boys were rewarded.[45] The figure covered in green boughs, as just described, was a central character in the springtime festivities throughout Britain and much of Europe. Known variously as the Green Man, Jack in the Green, Jack in the Bush, the Garland, Robin of the Wood, Robin Hood, May Man and King of the May, this enigmatic character embodies the idea of new life springing out of death, and he also brings the creative power of the tree spirit to the people.[46] The degree to which this concept permeates the whole of our mythology is indicated by the fact that such diverse figures as the mediaeval Wild Man of the Woods and the Green Knight of Arthurian legend (which has the theme of annual death and resurrection) also have their mythic origins here,[47] not to mention the foliate head found in church carvings, which has already been described in Chapter 5. St George, who elsewhere in Europe is known as Green George, is the

A traditional Jack in the Green is the centrepiece of this 1886 photograph.

same character in a slightly different guise. He, of course, appears in the Mummers' plays, and his saint's day is the spring date of 23 April.[48]

Traditionally in Britain, Jack in the Green (as we shall call him) was covered from head to foot by a wooden or wickerwork frame of roughly cone or pyramid shape which was left open at the bottom. This framework was covered with interwoven branches of greenery, flowers and ribbons so that the individual within was completely hidden, and only a peephole was left for him to see his way as he danced among the merrymakers.[49] The first recorded appearance of Jack in the Green is in the late eighteenth century when he was part of the group which celebrated the May festivities in London. The group included the Lord and Lady of the May, a fiddler and drummer, milkmaids and chimney sweeps.[50] The milkmaids had their own form of May garland which consisted of a pile of borrowed silver utensils and vessels, all highly polished and carried on their heads, or if too heavy and elaborate, carried separately.[51]

Why the chimney sweep should become the Jack in the Green might at first seem puzzling until we remember that the sweep is intimately connected with fire and ashes and it was the ashes of the sacred fires of earlier times which were thought to possess the fertilizing virtues and so were scattered over the fields.[52] Even today it is considered good luck (i.e. a good omen for future fertility) if a bride is met and kissed by a sweep, if he has just been working and has a blackened face. By the early nineteenth century the Jack in the Green was usually a sweep, and the Lord and Lady were other sweeps dressed in tawdry finery.[53] Their concern, however, was not the retention of old traditions but the need to make ends meet during the slack trade of the summer months, and the collecting box was always well in evidence. Chimney sweeping in the nineteenth century was done by sending small boys up the flues to bring the soot down and despite various public protests and attempts at legislation the practice continued until 1875 when the suffocation of a fourteen-year-old boy shocked the public conscience sufficiently. Towards the end of the century the sweeps' May festivities, including Jack in the Green, diminished.[54]

But the spirit of Jack in the Green is not entirely dead in Britain. At Castleton in Derbyshire, Garland Day is celebrated on 29 May, and perhaps this green man owes his survival to the fact that his parade was grafted on to the celebration of the return to the throne of Charles

A chimney sweep as Jack in the Green, depicted on a Devon inn-sign.

II in 1660. On this May evening the Garland King, wearing Stuart costume and seated on horseback, is covered by the beehive-shaped garland made of wild flowers and greenery. He is followed by the 'Lady' on a horse, a group of girls carrying posies, and Morris dancers, with a silver band at the rear. They stop at each of the six local pubs, where music and dances are performed. At the church the garland is removed and hoisted to the top of the tower where it remains for a week.[55]

Once May has ended, the seeds have been sown and the crops are growing. Then follow the major fertility rituals concerned with harvesting the produce, which we have already described in Chapter 8. But many other traditional customs have fertility overtones, and we shall describe some of them in the following chapter.

Castleton Garland Day, 1973.

11 Traditional customs with fertility overtones: water, sun, horses, horns, and she-males

'It must not be assumed that the cults of the Earth Mother encourage immorality in the profane sense of the term. Sexual union and the orgy are rites celebrated in order to re-actualize primordial events.'

Mircea Eliade, *Myths, Dreams and Mysteries*[1]

In any discussion of fertility the power of the fertilizing waters cannot be ignored. It may be self-evident that water is a source of life and growth, and without it the land, the crops, the animals and mankind will perish. But symbolically water can also be seen as a potent fertilizing liquid, so that the scattering of water in some traditional customs does not necessarily imply a charm for the procurement of rain, but may be used to bring 'good luck' or fecundity to those upon whom it falls.[2] In many parts of Britain there was keen competition on New Year's morning to be the first to draw water from wells, ponds or streams. This water was called the 'Flower' or 'Cream' of the well and would bring the drawer 'good luck' for the coming year. In Scotland it was given to cows to drink to increase their milk yield, and in Herefordshire a farm servant would present it to her mistress in return for a gift of money. If it was kept in the house it would protect the household during the coming year, but an unmarried girl would keep it herself and would expect to be married during the next twelve months. In Scotland the 'Cream of the Well' was brought into the house in silence, a little was drunk by each person, and every room and byre was sprinkled with it.[3]

There was a similar New Year custom which was practised until about the turn of this century, principally in Pembrokeshire and other parts of South Wales. At about 3 or 4 o'clock on New Year's morning a group of youths would visit the houses in their neighbourhood carrying a vessel of fresh spring water and some twigs of an evergreen, such as box or holly. Anyone they met on the way was sprinkled on the face and hands with water flung from the evergreen branch, and inside each house they would sprinkle a little water in every room. Particular attention was paid to couples who had been married during the past year. They were liberally sprinkled with the spring water as they lay in bed. The youths were rewarded by the householders with a payment of half a crown or five shillings. As late as 1913 mothers in Kidwelly

Two Tenby (Dyfed) children photographed while water sprinkling on
1 January 1928.

would sprinkle the faces of their sleeping children on New Year's Day.[4]

Water sprinkling was also practised during some May Day customs. Although Padstow's 'Obby 'Oss still prances and swirls through the streets as vigorously as ever, he no longer visits Treator Pool near the town. In past years the 'Oss would wade in, 'drink', and sprinkle the assembly with water, for good luck.[5] In parts of Eastern Europe, Easter Monday is known as Ducking Monday and on this day the young men and women splash each other with water before starting their egg shackling, a custom we described earlier. Similarly in Devon and Cornwall May Day was known as 'Ducking' or 'Dippy' Day. Anyone who went out without wearing a buttonhole of hawthorn could be doused with water by the young lads, who claimed this right on 1 May.[6] In an earlier age the May festivities in southern Ireland included a band of Mummers, one of whom was a masked clown. He carried a pole which was covered at one end with shreds of cloth, somewhat resembling a mop. This he would dip into a convenient pool or puddle and liberally sprinkle all about him. As Ireland is noted for its abundant rainfall, this custom is less likely to have originally been a rain charm, but was evidently a symbolic distribution of the fertilizing waters.[7]

At harvest time the last sheaf of corn was ceremonially severed, as has already been described in Chapter 8. In parts of Wales, after the ritual in the cornfield one of the reapers would run with the 'neck' to the farmhouse where he was met by a maid with a bucket of water. If he could evade her and enter the house dry, he would claim a kiss, but if he failed he received the water over his head. Likewise in other localities the reapers on the Horkey Cart which brought in the last load of the harvest would be liberally doused with water by those waiting in the farmyard.

A still familiar contest which may have originated as a rain-making ceremony is the tug-of-war, where two teams pull at opposite ends of a rope. This used to take place in Burma where one team represented rain and the other drought, the rain team being allowed to win with the expectation that rain would then fall. A traditional tug-of-war was practised in Ludlow, Shropshire, on Shrove Tuesday, when the teams used a 36-yard-long rope with a blue knob on one end and a red knob on the other. The Reds tried to pull the rope into Mill Street, and if they succeeded they would dip the knobs into the River Teme. The Blues tried to pull it into the Bull Ring, and then dip the knobs into the

Three boys at Llangynwyd, Mid Glamorgan, collecting *calennig* some
time during the years 1904–10.

River Corve. However, the crowds became so unruly at this event that it was discontinued in 1851. At nearby Presteigne (in Radnorshire over the Welsh border) a similar custom continued until the end of the nineteenth century. One team would try to get the rope to Broad Street and the River Lugg. The importance of the river in these customs does suggest an ancient rain-making ceremony.[8] It is interesting to note that the North American Eskimos had a similar rope-pulling contest designed to influence the weather. This occurred at the approach of winter when two teams composed of those who were born in the summer, and those born in winter, would each pull on the end of a long sealskin rope. If the summer team won, fine weather would continue into the winter.[9]

The action of the sun as the prime promoter of vitality on earth cannot be doubted, and the widespread use of the ritual fire to celebrate the vital radiations or to enhance the sun's growing or waning powers has already been detailed. But there were also other sun-inspired customs, of which the Welsh New Year's gift or *calennig* was one. In the last century on 1 January the children would visit friends and neighbours carrying an apple (or sometimes an orange) decorated with leaves, nuts, cloves, oats or wheat and dusted with flour. At each house they would ask for food or money by singing a verse such as:

> Mi godais heddiw ma's o'm tŷ
> A'm cwd a'm pastwn gyda mi,
> A dyma'm neges ar eich traws,
> Sef llanw'm cwd â bara a chaws.

(I came today out of my house with a bag and sticks, my errand here is to fill my bag with bread and cheese.)[10]

The custom was also practised in Gloucestershire, Herefordshire and Worcestershire. The connection it has with the sun is not immediately obvious, but Wirt Sikes suggested that it referred to a solar myth which stemmed from what he liked to call 'Druidic days'. He wrote that:

In the three supporting sticks of the apple are seen the three rays of the sun, ⁄|\ , the mystic Name of the Creator; the apple is the round sun itself; the ⁄|\ evergreens represent its perennial life; and the grains of wheat, or oats, Avagddu's spears. Avagddu is the evil principle of darkness – hell, or the devil – with which the sun fights throughout the winter for the world's life.[11]

Cheese-rolling at Cooper's Hill. The cheese can be seen on the left.

At Eastertime there were many gatherings on hilltops for the purpose of egg-rolling or -trundling as described in the previous chapter. At some of these, oranges were rolled downhill too. On Good Friday at Dunstable Downs, Bedfordshire, hundreds of children still roll oranges down into Pascombe Pit,[12] and until recently children scrambled for oranges which were rolled down Martinsell Hill, Wiltshire,[13] which was a noted site for fairs within its prehistoric earthwork. An orange makes an excellent sun symbol, but its use as such cannot really be ancient as oranges were not imported into Britain before the Middle Ages.[14] Another possible sun-symbol is a round, yellow cheese, and at Cooper's Hill near Brockworth in Gloucestershire these are still ceremonially rolled down the steep slope and raced after by young men and women on Spring Bank Holiday Monday.[15] A flower-decked maypole stands on top of the hill, though the uneven ground is unsuitable for dancing. Cheeses were also rolled at Uffington when the white horse was cleaned.[16]

A springtime ceremony which contains evocative echoes of pre-Christian sun veneration later became connected with Palm Sunday before dying out in the middle of the twentieth century. It was known as 'Seeking the Golden Arrow', and took place on Palm Sunday on Pontesford Hill near Pontesbury in Shropshire. As late as the last century, large numbers of people would gather on the hilltop in the early morning to search for the mythical golden arrow, although no one was sure what it was or why they were looking for it. There are various vague explanations – stories of defrauded heirs, lost estates, or fairy curses to be lifted – but as in many other cases these are later accretions to what was originally a very ancient ceremony to welcome the rising sun from a sacred high point. The golden arrow was perhaps the first shaft of light seen from the rising sun. Sprigs were plucked from a solitary yew tree, and other green branches were added, perhaps symbolic of the sun's fertilizing powers. Later there was a race downhill to a stream, and the day continued with food and drink and good cheer.[17]

The custom of visiting sacred hilltops on Palm Sunday is recorded elsewhere, and in the nineteenth century the day was known as Fig Sunday. In the southern counties, Wiltshire, the Midlands and Yorkshire, fig-feasts were common on this day. The villagers from Avebury climbed Silbury Hill, Wiltshire's famous prehistoric mound which is in fact the largest man-made prehistoric mound in Europe, to eat fig cakes and drink water sweetened with sugar, while at nearby

Swallowhead Spring, the source of the River Kennet, the same practice took place.[18] Fig-feasts were also held on Dunstable Downs in Bedfordshire and at Kempton, Hertfordshire. On Fig Sunday children were given packets of figs first thing in the morning, and fig puddings and pies were eaten at the midday meal. To meet the great demand, fig fairs were held beforehand. On Fig Sunday, large, happy crowds would gather on the hilltops to eat figs and other good things and to toast each other with ale or cider. These gatherings faded at the end of the nineteenth century and figs had by the start of World War I ceased to be eaten as a Palm Sunday dish.[19] The fig is a universal symbol of fecundity, the tree combining 'symbols of both the masculine and feminine principles, the fig leaf being the male, the linga, and the fig the female, the yoni ... A basket of figs is fertility and represents woman as goddess or mother.'[20]

Carved and painted figures depicting a man wearing an animal disguise have been found on cave walls in Europe, and may be as old as 15,000 years. Perhaps the best known of these was discovered in the

A Palaeolithic cave painting which was probably intended to depict a man disguised as an animal.

Volp cavern of Les Trois Frères in the foothills of the Pyrenees at the beginning of this century, and is usually known as the 'Sorcerer' of Les Trois Frères.[21] The horned god continued to be a powerful religious symbol in northern Europe, as was the horse, and both of these symbols were extensively used by the Celts in Britain. There is little doubt that a continuous link exists between these early practices and the animal disguises we are about to discuss, and that they had the common aim of promoting fertility in man, earth and beast.[22]

The most frequent animal disguise recorded in Britain is the horse. The Hooden Horse frequently appeared in north and east Kent during the last century, either at midwinter or Samhain (1 November). The head was usually made from a horse's skull, but sometimes of wood, and was fixed to a pole which was held by a man who was draped in a blanket or sheet. The lower jaw was hinged so that the 'Hoodener' beneath the blanket could make it open and close with a snap. The bottoms of glass bottles were used as eyes, and the head was decorated with colourful ribbons. A 'groom' carrying a whip led the horse by a bridle, a 'jockey' tried to ride on its back, and they were accompanied by a 'Mollie', a man dressed as a woman, who carried a besom. The group also included a few musicians. This team went from house to house singing songs and carols, and bringing good cheer. The horse would snap its jaws and chase the young women and have to be restrained by the groom. They were rewarded with food, drink and money and then went on to the next call.

The origin of the word 'Hoodening' is unknown. It has been suggested that it stems from 'Wooden horse' or 'Woden's horse', or from 'Robin Hood's horse', but most likely it is derived from 'hooded', which refers to the covered figure of the Hoodener. There are thirty-three sites of Hooden Horse performances recorded in Kent, though the custom seems to have lapsed completely at the turn of the century. However it has been revived recently at Folkestone, Charing, and other places.[23]

In Cheshire the horse has attached himself to a Mummers' play usually known as the Soul Cakers' play. This was performed at the time of Hallowe'en or All Souls Day (1 November) and was part of the widespread tradition of soul caking when special cakes were made and given to groups of soulers who would go from house to house, singing either a straightforward begging song or a similar song with the addition of a plea for prayers for the dead. The soul cakers' play follows the form of the traditional Mummers' play of challenge, fight, death, and magical revival, as outlined in the previous chapter. There are some extra characters in the play, one of them being the horse which is called Dicky Tatton or Dick or the Dobby Horse or Young Ball, and it is a typical hooden horse which prances and stamps and has to be restrained from leaping at the ladies by its groom or driver. The only current performance of this soul caking play now takes place at Antrobus in Cheshire and is a 1926 revival after a lapse of some fourteen years. The team no longer visits the wealthier farms and big houses, but tours the pubs by car.[24]

In South Wales the horse, now rarely seen, was made with a white sheet and was known as Mari Llwyd, which is thought to mean 'Grey Mare'. An earlier name was 'Aderyn bee y llwyd', 'Bird with the Grey Beak', which might show a link between this custom and the beaked horse of the Celts, such as that cut in the turf on the hillside at Uffington in Oxfordshire. The Mari Llwyd visited houses around Christmas and into the New Year, and the party would be made up of several characters who might include the Leader, Sergeant, Merryman who played a fiddle, and Punch and Judy, both of whom were men with blackened faces. They would try to gain admittance to

The Antrobus soulers with their horse. Note the 'she-male' on the left (a term explained later in this chapter).

202

a house by singing traditional verses which were answered from within. After the preliminaries the verses became impromptu and each side would try to outdo the other in wit and sarcasm. The side which ran out of rhyming insults first had to give way, though the Mari Llwyd was usually admitted, but it is recorded that at the turn of the century some public houses hired a 'poet' for the evening to keep the Mari Llwyd at bay. If they entered the pub the team was entitled to free drinks. Inside the house the Mari Llwyd behaved in the same way as the Hooden Horse, paying particular attention to women, prancing and neighing and being restrained by the leader. Judy swept outside the house, the front steps and the hearth with her brush, and Punch would stir the fire with his poker. Sometimes he would rake the fire out if the occupants had failed to make him promise not to. Perhaps this tradition was a link with the ritual of extinguishing all the domestic fires before the purifying 'need fire' could be ignited.[25] The group would also sing and dance, Punch would beat time on the floor with his poker and kiss the girls and was then chased by Judy waving her broom. Then they all ate and drank and the Mari Llwyd team would depart with a final benediction such as:

The Mari Llwyd team calling at a house in Llangynwyd, Mid Glamorgan, during the first decade of the twentieth century.

> We wish you joy,
> To sustain a new year,
> While the man continues to ring a bell,
> May you prosper more every day.[26]

The bell may refer generally to church bells or perhaps a bell that Punch wore on his costume. As with many of these customs drunkenness and bad behaviour latterly took the place of the original good-humoured fun, and so the custom tended to fall into disrepute and disuse, but even yet there are a few places in Glamorgan and Carmarthen where the Mari Llwyd is still surviving, though the attendant figures are fewer and less elaborately costumed than before.[27]

Ireland had its ritual horses too, which were called Láir Bhán (White Mare), but few of these have been recorded. There must have been far more than the half-dozen which are known. East of Cork between Ballycottin and Trabolgan the Láir Bhán appeared at Hallowe'en, 31 October. The party went to each farmhouse blowing cows' horns and reciting verses, which proclaimed that the group were messengers of 'Muck Olla' who had provided prosperity for the farmer in the past year and would continue to do so if he were generous to them. The messengers were rewarded with gifts of farm produce which were later sold and the money divided between them. In County Kerry the Láir Bhán took part in the May Day processions and it appeared again around Christmas as part of the obscure ritual of Hunting the Wren.[28]

Earlier we wrote of the ceremonies of May Day, and among the characters appearing, along with the Morris dancers, would be the Hobby Horse. The traditional festivities have now practically disappeared, but there is one May Day horse which flourishes even now in full vigour, and this is the famous 'Obby 'Oss at Padstow in Cornwall. On the day before May Day, the town is decorated with flags and greenery and a maypole is set up in the town centre. In the dark early hours of May morning, groups of mayers traverse the town serenading the occupants of various houses with words suited to the individual and set to a traditional tune. At the Golden Lion Inn, for example, they sing:

> Rise up, Mr Hawken, and joy to you betide,
>   For summer is acome unto day.
> And bright is your bride that lies down by your side,
>   In the merry morning of May.[29]

One of the Padstow 'Obby 'Osses, with the teaser.

There are in fact two 'Osses, the Old 'Oss whose accompanying mayers wear all white clothes with red sashes or ribbons, and the Blue Ribbon 'Oss whose attendants are likewise dressed in white, but with blue decoration. The Blue 'Oss is the first to appear at 10 a.m., and an hour later the Red 'Oss dances out from the Golden Lion. The 'Oss is made of a circular frame about 6 feet across which is covered with black oilskin and is carried on the shoulders. A skirt of black oilskin drapes down from the circumference of the frame. At the front is a small carved horse's head and at the rear is a tail of horse hair. The operator, whose head projects from a hole in the centre of the 'Oss, wears a strangely painted mask with a tall pointed hat. In front of the 'Oss goes the Dancer or Teaser who waves a 'club' which is a small shield-shaped bat with a handle. His or her job is to dance and twist about in front of the 'Oss to encourage it to do likewise. This it does very successfully, and the 'Oss swirls, prances and leaps, barely missing the packed onlookers who line the narrow streets of this small fishing town. As he dances through the town the 'Oss is accompanied by the mayers dressed all in white who also dance with a jaunty, swaying and swooping movement in time to the haunting 'Obby 'Oss tune played on accordions, melodeons and throbbing drums. The onlookers shout "'Oss, 'Oss, wee 'Oss', and sometimes the 'Oss jumps towards a young woman and covers her with his skirt. This is taken to mean that she will soon have a husband or a baby, and in earlier times the inside of the skirt was smeared with blacking which came off on the recipient of this 'good luck'. Every so often the mood changes, the music becomes slow and sad, and the mayers sing:

> O where is St George, O where is he-O?
> He's out in his long boat all on the salt sea-O.
> Up flies the kite, down falls the lark-O,
> Aunt Ursula Birdhood she had an old yow,
> And she died in her own Park-O.[30]

The horse sinks down and 'dies', and the Teaser strokes it with the club. Then with a thunderous roll on the drums the horse leaps to life and the jaunty tune starts once more as the crowd sings:

> Unite and unite and let us all unite,
> For Summer is acome unto day,
> And whither we are going we will all unite,
> In the merry morning of May.[31]

Playing the part of either the horse or the Teaser is exhausting work and different members of the group of mayers take these parts during the day as the 'Osses parade through the town and along the quayside. In the evening the two 'Osses meet at the maypole and dance together and the proceedings end with a farewell song.[32]

Not far from Padstow, at Minehead in Somerset, another May Day horse appears. This one is more brightly coloured than the Padstow 'Osses, its long frame being covered with strips of coloured cloth and the hessian skirt which hangs to the ground is decorated with multi-coloured circles. It is accompanied by musicians and two Gullivers who collect money for charities. At one time the Gullivers were rather rough with people who did not give freely enough, and a special boot was carried with which to punish them. For a while they went out of favour, but recently they have reappeared minus the boot. As at Padstow, Minehead has two horses, the traditional Sailors' Horse and a more recent Town Horse.[33]

Some of the other animals which take part in annual ceremonies are horned, and a notable use of reindeer antlers occurs in the Horn Dance which still takes place at Abbots Bromley in Staffordshire each year early in September. Throughout the year, the horns, of which there are six pairs, are kept in the parish church and are removed only to be used on the day and thereafter are returned to the church. Besides the six horn dancers there are six other characters in the performance. These are the Hobby Horse, Maid Marian (a man dressed as a woman who carries a collecting ladle), a Fool (with a bladder on a stick), a Bowman (Robin Hood), a boy with a triangle, and a musician with an accordion. They meet in the early morning, collect the horns from the church and start on a 20-mile circuit of the area, stopping outside farms and cottages to perform the dance. Facing each other in two rows, the men hold the reindeer antlers at head level and the two rows prance forwards and back again, almost locking horns each time but eventually passing by with a dexterous twist of the horns. This is done several times and then they move into single file and circle and weave around until re-forming into two rows again. In the nineteenth century the tour of the neighbourhood was over 30 miles long and the whole ceremony took about four days to complete, but in this century events have been speeded up and when we saw them in 1979 the antlers which weigh from 16 to 25 pounds were loaded on to a trailer and driven to the next stopping place while the dancers went on foot. In the seventeenth century the dance took place around Christmas,

The Hobby Horse which accompanies the horn dancers at Abbots Bromley.

and this suggests that originally it was a winter solstice custom designed to renew the vigour and fertility of the dormant natural world.[34]

The Christmas Bull, also known as The Broad, only appeared in a few villages in the south Cotswolds in Gloucestershire and in Wiltshire. The head was sometimes a stuffed skin or might be a cardboard mask, and occasionally a hollowed and carved turnip or swede with a lighted candle inside was used. It had real horns and glass eyes and was held up on a pole while the performer was covered with a sheet or sacking. During the Christmas season the group, who wore no special clothes, would go round the houses carrying a wooden wassail bowl decorated with colourful ribbons and sprigs of evergreens. Some of The Broads appeared on their own, and a few toured with a group of Christmas Mummers. The 1914 War ended the appearances of The Broads and they seem never to have been revived.[35] Wassailing is itself an early custom, the word deriving from the Anglo-Saxon *wes hál* meaning 'be of good health'. The wassail bowl was filled with lamb's

The Abbots Bromley Horn Dance, 1979. Bringing up the rear are Maid Marian (a 'she-male') and the Fool.

wool, a drink made from hot ale, spices, sugar, eggs, thick cream and roast apples. It was ceremonially circulated around the company at Yuletide and healths were drunk. In later years wassailers carried the wassail bowl around the houses in the neighbourhood singing wassail songs and offering a drink from the bowl in return for a gift of food or drink.[36]

In villages around Sheffield on the South Yorkshire–Derbyshire border there was the Christmas tradition of the Old Tup, which was similar to the Hooden Horse but had a sheep's head instead of a horse's. This head was usually made of wood and often had a real pair of horns fastened on to it. Old Tup appeared with a group of characters who performed a traditional hero-combat play where the Butcher stuck his knife into Old Tup who was then brought back to life by the Doctor. Other characters were Beelzebub, the Old Man and the Old Woman, who was, as usual, played by a man with a blackened face and who sometimes carried a broom.[37]

A carved and painted wooden mask from Melbury Osmond in Dorset depicted a terrifying human face with protruding eyes and

The Dorset Ooser.

large horns sprouting from the head. This was called the Ooser (pronounced 'wurser') and was designed to be worn on the performer's head while his body would probably have been covered in an ox hide or material to resemble such. There is no record of any ceremony connected with the Ooser, and the only known mask was lost in the early years of this century.[38]

Another celebration of the horned fertility god took place at Charlton in Kent until 1872. This was the Horn Fair on 18 October, St Luke's Day, whose emblem is the horned ox. Horns were worn or carried by everyone. All the stalls were decorated with them, and even the gingerbread was made in horn-stamped moulds. The local saying was that 'All's fair at Horn Fair', and inhibitions were relaxed as the men, who frequently wore women's clothing, struck the women with pieces of furze. Water was liberally thrown about and there was much bawdy horseplay. The Horn Fair at Ebernoe in Sussex, which still takes place on 25 July, is a rather more sober affair. The central theme here is the roasting of a whole horned sheep, during which a cricket match is played. The cricket teams eat the roast meat for lunch and at

The captain of the Ebernoe cricket team bastes the sheep during the Horn Fair.

211

the end of the day the highest scorer of the winning team takes the horns as a trophy.[39] There is also a ram-roasting each Spring Bank Holiday Monday at Kingsteignton in Devon. This open-air roasting is accompanied by sports and maypole dancing, and later the roast meat is distributed among the assembled crowd. There are records of other ram roastings in Devon which took place in the last century, but they have now ceased.[40]

Readers who have followed our narrative so far will doubtless have been noting the indications of fertility practices that are evident in the foregoing. Both the horse and the horned god were potent figures in Celtic mythology and ritual, and we have no hesitation in suggesting that the ritual animal figures we have been describing have direct, though sometimes tenuous, links stretching back to the time when the

A carving of a horned figure discovered at the Roman fort of Alauna (Maryport) in Cumbria.

Celtic culture was dominant in the British Isles. Epona was a Celtic horse goddess whose attributes included fecundity and maternity, and across Europe, wherever they settled, the Celts left traces of their veneration of the horse ranging from small bronzes to the 360-foot chalk carving of the white horse on the hillside at Uffington.[41] The hobby horse of recent centuries was recognized and welcomed as a bringer of fertility to humans, animals and the earth, and this was displayed by its prancing vitality and its attentions directed at the young women who would expect to gain a husband or baby soon afterwards. This aspect of its powers is still evident at Padstow in the May Day celebrations, as are its death and resurrection, a theme that also appears in the Mumming plays that are associated with the horse, and relate to the annual recycling of life as evidenced in the natural

The so-called 'Beechamwell demon' is thought to have been carved about 1340 when a south aisle was added to the old Saxon church at Beechamwell in Norfolk. The drawing on the left shows more clearly that the figure is horned, carries what is possibly a piece of foliage, and has his tongue sticking out. All three characteristics point to the figure being a fertility symbol.

world. The Irish Láir Bhán in particular brought a direct promise of fertility and prosperity to the farms it visited.[42] The cult of the horned god was also widespread among the Celts in Europe and Britain, and he was frequently depicted in carvings and metalwork, with antlers, bull's horns or ram's horns. In all cases he was understood to be a bringer of fertility and this aspect was emphasized especially in Brigantia in the north-east of Britain, where horned figures with phallus have been found.[43] The rites of the horned god were widely practised and of great antiquity when the Christian missionaries were spreading across Europe, and they saw it as their duty to suppress and discredit the old gods in order to promote the new. They considered the people's unashamed celebration of fecundity repugnant and

An old engraving shows the traditional anti-witchcraft view of the witches' horned god, or Devil.

repeatedly denounced such practices. In the ninth century AD, it was proclaimed that 'If any one at the Kalends of January goes about as a stag or a bull, that is, making himself into a wild animal, and putting on the heads of beasts; those who in such wise transform themselves into the appearance of a wild animal, penance for three years, because this is devilish.'[44] And so, in the simplest terms, the ancient horned god of fertility became the horned satanic figure of the Christian Devil.

Throughout the fertility customs we have been describing, the figure of the man dressed as a woman (more conveniently referred to as a 'she-male') very frequently appears. With the Kent Hooden Horse came the Mollie with her besom, in Wales the Mari Llwyd horse was accompanied by Judy who also carried a besom, while the broom-carrying she-male with the Old Tup players from the Sheffield area was called Our Old Lass. The Abbots Bromley Horn Dance she-male is now known as Maid Marian and her emblem of office is a ladle, while at the Horn Fair at Charlton any man could appear dressed in women's clothes. On May Day the London sweeps celebrated with the Lord and Lady, the Lady of course being a she-male, and on the

A Plough Monday procession in Yorkshire, including a 'she-male' in dress, apron, and frilly cap.

The Goathland (North Yorkshire) Plough Stots, held on the first Saturday after Plough Monday, includes a team of sword dancers and a 'Betty', seen here. 'She' carries a collecting box and a broom.

Bob Williams, the last 'Cadi' from Holywell in Clwyd, photographed
some time before 1939.

Isle of Man in the May Day battle between the forces of the Queen of May and the Queen of Winter, the latter was also a she-male. The ceremony of Plough Monday was accompanied by the Bessie, and even today at the Ickwell May Day festivities in Bedfordshire the Moggies, a she-male and 'her' husband, can still be seen.[45]

The she-male is not exclusive to Britain, for he/she appears throughout the history of folk customs worldwide. The besom that many she-males carried was recognized as a symbol of sexuality.[46] Traditionally the she-male has a blackened face, sometimes with reddened lips, cheeks and eye sockets, or 'she' might occasionally wear a mask instead. This disguise would enable a known individual in a small community fully to assume the role of the mythic character and so more effectively carry out the function assigned to that character. Ritual transvestism is of some antiquity, as can be seen from the following quotation dated to around AD 400.

Behold the days come, behold the kalends come, and the whole devilish public procession goes forth. The new year is consecrated with old blasphemies. Whatever deformities are lacking in nature, which creation does not know, art labours to fashion. Besides, people are dressed as cattle, and men are turned into women.[47]

But the she-male should not be viewed simply as tomfoolery or licentiousness. The transsexual disguise was originally an attempt to encompass the nature of the Ultimate Godhead itself. By definition the first cause must encompass everything and every polarity, including male and female, and from this springs the first creative act. The she-male character is not representing the female aspect of this duality but is being the totality itself. In North Wales the principal character of the May dance was the Cadi who combined the qualities of 'marshal, orator, buffoon and money collector'. The upper half of his body was dressed as a man, but from the waist down he wore petticoats.[48] In more immediate fertility terms the she-male can be seen as symbolizing the union between the cosmic energies of the sky father and the telluric energies of the earth mother, thus aiding the formation of the fertilizing energies which needed to be channelled throughout the land.

12 Earth energies and the maintenance of fertility

'The Earth is indeed a living being. If we relate to her harmoniously, respecting her etheric organs, she will speak to us, inspire us, nourish us, work and co-operate with us.'

Adam McLean[1]

In this book we have attempted to trace the theme of fertility through the ages, from prehistory to the present day. We consider that the evidence shows that fertility was always of paramount importance, until materialism began to dominate the thoughts of Western man, and that all that remains of the ancient fertility practices are the few traditional customs which, though having lost their real meaning, are still performed today. But were these customs ever anything more than quaint rural ways of passing the time? How can we be sure that our interpretation is correct? Did the rituals so vigorously performed have any real effect, or did they merely demonstrate the hopes of the performers for rain and sun, healthy crops and cattle? We believe the evidence indicates that not only were our ancestors very much aware of what their rituals were designed to achieve, but also that they were utilizing energies which are now unknown to us. That, in fact, they were not the primitive savages or dull peasants as seen by 'enlightened' modern man, but were in harmony with their surroundings and were able to live contented lives untroubled by the ills of the twentieth century. Lest we be accused of seeing the past through a romantic haze, we should add that we are fully aware that there has always been inequality, injustice and suffering, and never more so than today, but in natural societies where the people were able to live close to nature the sickness and mental and emotional disorientation which are now sweeping over mankind could never occur. In Britain today there is little difference between the country dweller and the urbanite, both having been wooed by urban ideals and eating the same unnatural foods, watching the same stultifying television programmes and having the same materialistic outlook on life. And yet, not everyone is trapped into believing that humanity is progressing rapidly towards perfection, that the past was awful and the future can only be better. Some people are trying to rediscover man's forgotten past, studying the clues and interpreting the scanty

219

information retrieved. The findings are startling, especially with regard to the unknown energy sources about which we have been writing.

Antiquarians in past centuries studied prehistoric sites and in the absence of facts they attributed them to the Romans or peopled them with Druids. Twentieth-century archaeologists, limited by their own materialist world-view, designate the remains as burial or ritual sites, and despite the assistance of current technology have been unable or unwilling to probe any further. A significant advance in the study of prehistory began in the 1920s when Alfred Watkins set out the theory of leys in his classic book *The Old Straight Track*.[2] Although he appeared to be convinced that the alignments he had discovered (straight lines linking sites of antiquity such as standing stones and other prehistoric sites, crosses, old churches, holy wells, and also certain crossroads, sacred trees, and mountain tops) were evidence of a network of trackways crisscrossing the country and nothing more, his new way of looking at the countryside was to lead to developments beyond his wildest imaginings, developments which are still in train today. The next major step forward was the appearance in 1969 of an inspired book, *The View Over Atlantis* by John Michell.[3] Having studied Watkins's work and the Chinese beliefs involving dragon paths or *lung mei*, Michell intuitively drew together many threads into a logical pattern which has been the starting point for many people's active interest in 'earth mysteries' during the past ten years. As he wrote in *The View Over Atlantis*: 'all the evidence from the remote past points to the inescapable conclusion that the earth's natural magnetism was not only known to men some thousands of years ago,

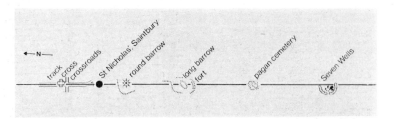

A plan of the Saintbury ley, Gloucestershire, which runs for about 3½ miles north-north-west to south-south-east on the northern edge of the Cotswold Hills.

An aerial view of the Saintbury ley, looking south.

but it provided them with a source of energy and inspiration to which their whole civilization was tuned.'[4]

Watkins's early work on leys has now been refined and extended,[5] and with the introduction of dowsers with their psychic sensitivities and scientists with their delicate measuring instruments into the field, the knowledge of the energies present in leys and at ancient sites is increasing, though the subject's complexity tends to grow as more is learned. But before we investigate these recent developments let us first re-examine some of the traditional customs and see what links they may have with leys and energy production or utilization. We have already suggested that the many customs involving dancing (for example Morris dancing, May Day dancing, dancing around bonfires) and skipping may have been intended to raise energy, and this idea can be extended to the rowdy and boisterous games which are also such a feature of Britain's traditions. A few examples are the Shrovetide football games ('football of the old, wild type')[6] which were once widely played and still are at Sedgefield in Durham, Alnwick in

Shrove Tuesday football being played in the river at Ashbourne, 1921.

Morris men in action during the Aston-on-Clun Arbor Day festivities in Shropshire, 1980.

Northumberland, Atherstone in Warwickshire and Ashbourne in Derbyshire; Easter ball-games like 'stoolball, knurr-and-spell, trapball, ninepins, hand ball, bowls and football';[7] the violent Haxey Hood Game already described in Chapter 7; the equally frightening Bottle-Kicking at Hallaton in Leicestershire on Easter Monday;[8] and Whuppity Stourie, which takes place on 1 March at Lanark and formerly involved a stand-up fight.[9] There are many others, not only in Britain, and as Mircea Eliade comments: 'The contests and fights which take place in so many places in the spring or at harvest time undoubtedly spring from the primitive notion that blows, contests, rough games between the sexes and so on, all stir up and increase the energies of the whole universe.'[10]

The customs may become clearer if we instead describe them as magical rites performed to raise energy, which is then directed to the desired goal, which is usually the fructification of crops, cattle, people, and the well-being of the land itself. When these magical rites are performed at prehistoric sites which themselves may already produce or store energy, then the rites are adding to the energies present at the site and available for use. With our scanty knowledge of the earth's energy network, we do not know how many customs were performed

In the thick of the Hallaton bottle-kicking.

at energy sites which were known to the performers but are no longer obvious as such. There is however some real evidence that customs *were* held at ancient energy sites. In Cumbria, Easter and May Day games and sports were held in ancient earth circles like the Broomsgill ring and King Arthur's Round Table.[11]. Throwl-egg was played on Shrove Tuesday at barrows near Wold Newton (North Yorkshire) and Driffield (Humberside),[12] while on Good Friday the people of Linton and Hildersham in Cambridgeshire used to meet at the seven Romano-British barrows at Bartlow for 'skipping at the Hills'.[13] Skipping on burial mounds was done elsewhere on Palm Sunday or Good Friday, as on the barrows near Hove and Alciston in East Sussex.[14] At one time ball-games were regularly played in or outside churches, and we have already described the Cardiff tennis-ball game in Chapter 10.

The widespread customs of partaking of fig cakes, sugared water or liquorice water usually took place on the summits of sacred hills, such as Silbury Hill, at prehistoric sites, or at holy wells. At Fortingall in Tayside the Samhain bonfire was built on the Bronze Age barrow called Carn nam Marbh (the Mound of the Dead),[15] and in Guernsey a cup-marked rock called La Roque Balan in the parish of the Vale was the location of a large annual bonfire until the early nineteenth century. The local people would also gather there for dancing on the eve of St John's Day.[16] On the same day, St John's Stone in Abbey Fields, Leicester, was visited by the people.[17] On May Eve a maypole was erected in the Frying Pan, a small earthwork above the Cerne Abbas Giant in Dorset, and the usual festivities were held there on 1 May.[18] Old May Day (13 May) was the day for celebrations at Durrington in Wiltshire, a maypole topped by a newly cut may bush being chained to an old stone cross by the churchyard, and a feast and dancing held there.[19] Fairs were often held at ancient sites. In Lincolnshire the village fair at Thoresby was held near the church in a field containing a large bluestone,[20] but often the fairs were held on hills, such as Martinsell Hill (where there are prehistoric earthworks) in Wiltshire, the site of an annual fair, and in the same county also Yarnbury Castle (within the hillfort), Westbury Hill (above the white horse, where there is a hillfort and a barrow), and Cold Berwick Hill.[21] In Ireland a fair was held at a fort at Cnocan near Mallow in County Cork until about 1870,[22] and until recently there was dancing at a cairn on the summit of Slieve Croob in County Down on the first Sunday in August (Blaeberry Sunday).[23]

Since most ancient sites can be shown to be sited on leys, or energy networks, there is obviously a strong link between traditional customs and energy sites, a link which diligent research could no doubt strengthen. Jeremy Harte has already noted that the Alnwick Shrove Tuesday football game takes place along the main street, the A1068, which aligns with a church, an abbey, and Eglingham church, while part of the A351 road in Corfe Castle, Dorset, again where Shrovetide football is played, aligns with the castle and a tumulus.[24]

Before we look at the work being done today to isolate and identify the energies present at ancient sites and leys, let us summarize our personal interpretation of the true purpose of some of the traditional customs (and before them, the rituals performed by our prehistoric ancestors). We strongly suspect that originally, before the rituals degenerated, the participants were intending to *produce energy*, either by mental means, focusing their minds on the desired result in an attempt to achieve it, or by physical means, dancing or other active

A 1951 photograph of quarrymen playing football at Corfe Castle along the road that forms part of the ley. The castle, also on the ley, dominates the town.

movement to raise energy; or to *manipulate energy* which they knew could be tapped at ancient sites or similar foci along the energy network. Whether readers can accept these concepts depends on how aware they are of the current research being undertaken in Britain into the energies found at ancient sites and along leys.

Once it was suspected that energy in some form was present, the biggest contribution in the search for it was initially made by dowsers. Although many people connect dowsing with water divining, today its applications are much wider. Dowsing has been used in archaeological research since at least the 1930s,[25] the best-known dowser in this field being Guy Underwood who published *The Pattern of the Past* describing his work.[26] To the uninitiated, his water lines, track lines, aquastats, blind springs, primary spirals, nodes, branch spirals and other subdivisions of the 'geodetic lines' he traced with his divining rod are difficult to comprehend, but some of his findings concerning the 'Earth Force' are relevant to our present search for the energies

The American Indians may have been able to utilize earth energies inside their kivas. This 1888–9 photograph by Matilda Coxe Stevenson shows a sick boy being treated by five male members of the Medicine Division of the Giant Society at Sia Pueblo, New Mexico.

which may have been utilized by our ancestors. He discovered that animals are sensitive to the 'Earth Force', this being demonstrated by their practice of giving birth on blind springs ('centres upon which primary lines converge, and from which they emerge'),[27] and he gives many examples of this. He concludes that the places chosen 'must have a health-giving or restorative property which is instinctively recognized by the animal kingdom', and tells how old campaigners in the Peninsular Wars always chose, when sleeping rough, to lie where a cow had lain because by doing so they avoided getting rheumatics.[28] Underwood's finding was confirmed by Paul Devereux and Ian Thomson when they were doing their fieldwork for *The Ley Hunter's Companion*. In Herefordshire they found a moated mound on which, according to the farmer, the cows often chose to have their calves.[29] Following much intensive dowsing at prehistoric sites, churches and cathedrals, Underwood concluded that the positions and layouts of such sites were actually determined by the geodetic lines to be found there, but later dowsers dispute his theories, which they consider to be 'too rigid',[30] while agreeing with his observations.

Guy Underwood worked solely with underground patterns, whereas later dowsers have located effects above ground, which Tom Graves refers to as 'overgrounds'. Standing stones have been found to carry 'charges' (the nature of the force or energy is still unknown, hence the difficulty in naming it) which are sometimes so powerful that the dowser is thrown back from a stone when he touches it.[31] Also, pulses of energy have been measured travelling from stone to stone around a stone circle, and long distances across country as overgrounds from one site to another. These overgrounds, Tom Graves feels, are 'the semi-physical or non-physical reality behind leys',[32] and he reports that an overground 'resembles an amplitude-modulated laser beam, precisely straight for any length from a few feet to many miles, often less than six feet wide for its entire length, and at (so far) any height from ground level upwards.'[33] It is impossible to encapsulate in this chapter all Tom Graves's findings, since he has been extremely active in the field of leys and dowsing, and anyone wishing to learn the whole story is urged to read his exciting book *Needles of Stone*. We will here concern ourselves solely with those findings that relate specifically to the theme of this book. An important one is Graves's use of the Chinese system of acupuncture to help explain the working of the network of standing stones in Britain. Just as an acupuncturist uses needles inserted at specific points on the human body to control the energy flow, in the same way in earth-acupuncture standing stones ('needles of stone') were placed to control the flow of earth energy.[34] Tom Graves sees holy wells as needles in reverse, 'a needle of nothing connecting the energies of the water to the outside air',[35] and the pagan bonfires as 'needles of fire' paralleling the acupuncture practice of moxibustion, or the application of heat at selected points.[36] Maypoles were 'needles of wood', with energy being produced by dancing, the energy being 'primed and directed by the state of mind of the participants in the dancing'.[37]

Dowsers today can locate the energy pulses at and travelling between ancient sites by means of dowsing rods and pendulums. These are in effect ways of focusing their own innate sensitivity and some dowsers use only their hands for dowsing. This being so, and remembering that animals too are naturally sensitive to the earth's emanations, there is little doubt that our ancestors, who lived in greater harmony with the earth than we do, were able to sense easily

Leslie Banks (*right*) dowsing at the Rollright Stones, Oxfordshire, his progress being monitored by Geoff Blundell, developer of the Mind Mirror EEG device.

the ebb and flow of the earth's pulses, energies, forces, charges – whatever we care to call them. If this is accepted as a fact, then many mysteries of the past are on the way to being solved. The theories of leys, energies at ancient sites, and man's use of these energies, all seem eminently logical. Not so easy to ascertain, however, is the exact nature of the energies, how they are formed and what governs their movement. A scientific approach to these problms is being taken, and to this end the Dragon Project has been set up, comprising a group of people covering a wide range of disciplines, from inorganic chemistry to psychic research. Practical work began in the autumn of 1978, when a programme of monitoring the prehistoric sites at Rollright in Oxfordshire started, chief co-ordinator being Dr G. V. Robins. Not until 1980 was round-the-clock monitoring possible, but from mid-February to mid-March 1980, a minimum of eight hours a day physical monitoring was carried out, involving ultrasonic detection, microwave monitoring, electric field detection, geiger monitoring, and experimental infra-red photography. There was also experimentation involving dowsing and clairvoyance. At the time of writing, the Dragon Project is still in action and no conclusions have been reached,[38] but in a report published early in 1980 Dr Robins made some tentative comments on the possible implications of the Project, including:

... it seems that ancient man must have had an awareness – at whatever level – of the energy exchange system involved and sought to manipulate it, although for what ends we are not sure. Two possibilities that have emerged are the healing effect associated with weak electric fields, and the enhanced grain germination rates achieved with some ultrasonic frequencies, but this analysis of uses has barely begun.[39]

It can be seen then that the pioneering research being carried out by the members of the Dragon Project has far-reaching implications, and if the final conclusions bear out the early findings, a massive upheaval in present-day thinking about our ancestors will be unavoidable.

So far we have followed dowsers' and scientists' clues to ley energy. There are also other paths to follow which may prove fruitful. The first involves quartz, a substance we have already noted in *The Secret Country* as being widely found in the stones used in stone circles.[40] In that book we described folklore traditions relating to the use of quartz at ancient sites, and Dr G. V. Robins has explored the properties of quartz in an attempt to work out why it is seen so often. He concluded

'The White Stone', a magnificent 6-foot quartz standing stone at Cregg, County Londonderry.

that 'the materials chosen for alignment sites have well established physical properties which might allow energy to be stored, concentrated and amplified.'[41] Very many ancient sites have survived to our present technological age and it is incredible that so little scientific experimentation is being carried out in this exciting field. There is no need to look to outer space for new scientific discoveries, for there is an unsolved mystery here at home. Theories like that put forward for the use of quartz in stone circles should be tested with all the sophisticated tools at man's disposal, instead of dedicated enthusiasts having to devote their spare time and money to this research; but perhaps the Establishment would prefer not to be faced with incontrovertible revolutionary findings that would necessitate a rewriting of the history books and archaeological manuals.

Unknown energies are not exclusive to the 'earth mysteries' field. The history of psychical research is littered with theories postulating new forms of energy to explain apparently inexplicable phenomena, such as telepathy (mind-to-mind communication), psychokinesis or telekinesis (the movement of objects by non-physical means), and poltergeists. A poltergeist manifests itself by the unusual behaviour of familiar objects: furniture moves around the room, small objects whizz through the air from nowhere, children are thrown out of bed, and so on. Everything that happens in a poltergeist outbreak involves the use of energy, but no one is really sure what sort of energy or how it is employed, despite the fact that poltergeists have been a familiar nuisance since at least AD 530.[42] Usually there is an adolescent, or a mentally or emotionally disturbed person, in the household plagued by the poltergeist, and it is generally agreed among researchers that the energy somehow emanates from them, or is unknowingly directed by them. This was the case in a recent, well-witnessed, 'classic' poltergeist outbreak at Enfield near London, about which an enthralling book has been written.[43]

It is not known whether the energy manifested in poltergeist outbreaks is the same as that used by people who are able to move objects without touching them. In the case of the Russian lady, Madame Nelya Mikhailova (also known by her maiden name, Ninel Kulagina), her PK (psychokinetic) ability is indisputable since she has performed many times in laboratory conditions and around sixty films have been made of her moving objects simply by gazing at them or moving her hands above them. In 1971 a new PK performer burst upon the world, the controversial Uri Geller. He too performed before cameras, bending metal objects with ease merely by stroking them or concentrating on them. His powers did not fail when he was subjected to scientific tests, and he was also able to move the needles of geiger-counters and other instruments. Following the worldwide publicity he generated, other people discovered that they had similar abilities, especially children, and the most talented were scientifically studied. In 1973 a long-term PK experiment was begun in Toronto, Canada, and a group of psychic researchers had overwhelming success in creating a fictitious character they named Philip. In regular meetings they built up his personality, and finally he took on a kind of life,

Stanislawa Tomczyk of Poland, displaying her PK ability in 1913.

rapping in answer to questions, moving the table, and creating more problems than he solved.[44] The relevance of 'Philip', psychokinesis and poltergeists to our discussion of the energy possibly employed by our ancestors is that these phenomena are fact, and there can be no disputing their reality. So, having established that the human mind can cause the apparently impossible energy manipulations which are seen in psychokinesis and poltergeist outbreaks, there is no logical reason why other forms of energy cannot also be controlled and manipulated to bring about the desired results, which, in the case of our ancestors, would have been the fertility and well-being of crops, people and the land. There is in fact modern evidence to suggest that human energy emanations can affect rainfall and plant growth.[45]

The scientists working on the Dragon Project have established links between the energies they have monitored and the phases of the moon,[46] which is interesting in view of the fact that the moon has long been held to play an important role in certain aspects of human fertility: 'We find the symbolism of spirals, snakes and lightning – all of them growing out of the notion of the moon as the measure of rhythmic change and fertility – in the Siberian cultures of the Ice Age.'[47] The ovulation or fertility cycle of the human female is about a month long, leading people to believe that it must at one time have been somehow linked to the phases of the moon, and there are also other clear connections between the moon and the fertility of living things.[48] The old beliefs about the right times to perform agricultural tasks indicate an ancient knowledge, possibly instinctive, of the effects of outside influences on life on earth. It was not only the moon that affected the crops. According to Maria Thun, who has spent over twenty-five years researching into the effects of extra-terrestrial influences on plant life, 'Long observation has shown that forces coming from the fixed stars beyond the Moon's orbit work in differentiated ways upon the Earth and into the soil and through this have also an influence on the plant.'[49] In her book on her research, there is an emphasis on the natural and universal rhythms, and there is every likelihood that these rhythms have long been known to mankind, which may explain why certain rituals were performed at fixed times each year.

The serpent is a lunar symbol, also connected with woman and fecundity, though the link is complex,[50] and it also symbolizes energy. Indeed in its dragon form it was intimately bound up with the lore of earth energies, as we attempted to show in our earlier book *The Secret*

Country.[51] The serpent has raised its head from time to time in the preceding chapters – in the St Bride's Day poem quoted in Chapter 1, and in the Maryport Serpent Stone illustrated in Chapter 4, for example – and there are other ways in which the symbol is relevant to our theme. 'Serpent energy' may have been symbolized on the ground by the construction of serpentine avenues, such as those believed to have formerly existed at Avebury, and along these avenues the people

The Norman crypt beneath Lastingham church in North Yorkshire is a powerful energy site, where many ley researchers including the authors have experienced overwhelming energy emanations. Paul Devereux and Ian Thomson describe a ley passing through the church in their *Ley Hunter's Companion*. When there, we found several serpent carvings in the crypt, including those illustrated on the following page, which were beside the chancel where we experienced the strongest energies. Coincidence? Or a symbol of the power of the site?

236

would once have processed, generating energy (as in serpentine dances) as they moved towards the stone circles where, according to Michael Dames, they then engaged in powerful fertility rites in the Avebury Wedding Ring.[52]

Apart from describing and illustrating some traditional customs which have survived to the present day, we have of necessity dwelt in the past throughout this book. But just because the system of energy production and utilization has been forgotten does not mean that it is no longer possible to reactivate it, or that energy is no longer being produced naturally and stored in the standing stones and ley network. The earth continues to live despite man's abandonment of his supporting role. And incredibly, without realizing it, man seems to be actually perpetuating the ley system, even extending it. Work by dowsers suggests that the construction of modern structures such as microwave towers is creating new leys which are active.[53] So despite man's interference in innumerable ways, there is energy aplenty which could, if channelled correctly, be used to benefit all life on this

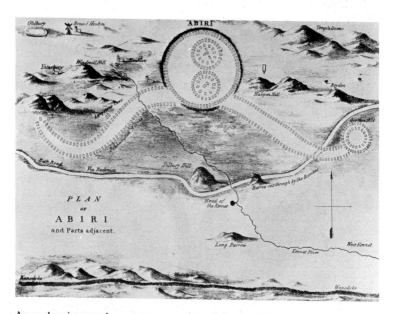

An early-nineteenth-century engraving of the Avebury area, showing the avenues first seen as serpentine by eighteenth-century antiquarian Dr William Stukeley.

planet. Today man seems to delight in energy-*draining* activities. Noise is energy-draining, the modern pace of life is energy-draining, the gabble-talk of radio is energy-draining, watching a TV screen is energy-draining. In our entertainments, as Bob Stewart here describes, twentieth-century man re-enacts pagan practices but with an ironic reversal – they are energy-draining instead of life-enhancing.

The images of the mass media are fundamentally expressions of the gods and goddesses. Any witness to a mass concert of popular music will realize the close similarity to orgiastic worship as described classically – the pounding rhythms, the sexual music, the use of drugs, the mass release of inhibitions through submersion in the group-mind are all typical aspects. Dominating the entire pattern are the cult figures of the artists, performing well-rehearsed sounds and motions to excite and command the energies of their devotees. This is the giant-scale contemporary version of the ritual behaviour of the ancient world, where priests and priestesses utilized the energies of the people to bring the community closer to the Mother Goddess or to her Son. Today those energies are unscrupulously drained away for the purposes of profit, with no return or sense of life-participation being offered.[54]

The Great Serpent Mound, Ohio, U.S.A., is 1,254 feet long and averages 20 feet across. It is one of many earthworks built by the American Indians over 2,000 years ago.

It is becoming increasingly evident to many people that our currently unbalanced materialist attitudes to life are producing a spreading and deep-seated sickness in humanity. The technology which increasingly dominates our lives should in fact be one useful method among many which could be used to solve our problems, and individuals, instead of becoming ever more dependent upon authority as is happening now, should seek to develop their own innate abilities, take charge of their own lives, and find a more balanced and holistic way of life. We do not advocate a return to the past, even if that were possible, but we do suggest that humanity must try to rediscover the life-enhancing values which our ancestors understood and lived by.

There are some small, hopeful indications that this is happening. The movements towards a return to the land and self-sufficiency, organic cultivation of crops, vegetarian and wholefood diets, the practice of handicrafts, and the research being conducted into the production of energy from non-polluting and renewable sources such as sun, wind and water, all indicate a new and positive approach to the material problems of life. Also, the growing interest in eastern philosophies and the development of the new pagan movement indicate the increasing search for a valid and satisfying spiritual life. But a danger occurs when these movements are noticed and seized upon by the voracious media, who all too often are only interested in providing entertainment. A serious trend then becomes merely 'trendy' and fashionable, and after a brief meteoric vogue is cast aside by the media as no longer newsworthy. Individuals who briefly adopt 'new' ideas in order to appear in fashion are simply amusing themselves, and in reality nothing changes. The person who really feels a need to reassess his or her own attitude to life will usually start from a profound distaste for the life attitudes which society presents as being worthy and admirable, and in the search for an alternative will be guided towards some of the 'new' ideas already mentioned.

Humanity is now faced with a choice of two paths. We can continue in our present mode of behaviour towards increasing physical and mental sickness and greater alienation from the planetary ethos and thus eventually destroy ourselves. Or there can be a radical reawakening to the realization that the health and vitality of our planet earth and the life forms upon her surface are intimately connected and that mankind has the innate power to influence his environment not only by physical but also by mental means. If these concepts were to be understood and followed, there would be a revolutionary change in

239

everyone's behaviour. Many of the present concerns and activities of humanity would be seen as pointless, if not decidedly dangerous, and men and women would at last be free to devote their energies to the true purpose of their incarnation in this world.

The portents suggest that the final choice will have been made by the year 2000. We look forward with interest to the twenty-first century.

Bibliography

Allegro, John, *Lost Gods*, London: Michael Joseph, 1977; London: Abacus Books, 1978

Burl, Aubrey, *Rites of the Gods*, London: J. M. Dent & Sons, 1981

Dames, Michael, *The Silbury Treasure*: The Great Goddess Rediscovered, London: Thames & Hudson, 1976

Dames, Michael, *The Avebury Cycle*, London: Thames & Hudson, 1977

Eliade, Mircea, *Patterns in Comparative Religion*, London: Sheed & Ward, 1958

Frazer, Sir James George, *The Golden Bough*: A Study in Magic and Religion, abridged edition, London: Macmillan & Co., 1922

Gooch, Stan, *Guardians of the Ancient Wisdom*, London: Wildwood House, 1979; London: Fontana Books, 1980

Graves, Tom, *Needles of Stone*, London: Turnstone Books, 1978; London: Panther Books, 1980

Hole, Christina, *British Folk Customs*, London: Hutchinson Publishing, 1976; London: Paladin Books, 1978

McLean, Adam, *The Four Fire Festivals*, Edinburgh: Megalithic Research Publications, 1979

Michell, John, *The Earth Spirit*: Its Ways, Shrines and Mysteries, London: Thames & Hudson, 1975

Neumann, Erich, *The Great Mother*: An Analysis of the Archetype, Princeton, N.J.: Princeton University Press, second edition 1963

Pedler, Kit, *The Quest for Gaia*: A Book of Changes, London: Souvenir Press, 1979

Rawson, Philip, ed., *Primitive Erotic Art*, London: Weidenfeld & Nicolson, 1973

Ross, Anne, *Pagan Celtic Britain*: Studies in Iconography and Tradition, London: Routledge & Kegan Paul, 1967; London: Cardinal Books, 1974

Notes

Where only author and book title are given, publication details can be found in the Bibliography. The book page references relate to the first edition listed in the Bibliography, unless otherwise noted.

1 The Great Earth Mother

1. James Mooney, 'The Ghost-Dance Religion and the Sioux Outbreak of 1890', *Annual Report of the Bureau of American Ethnology* (Washington, 1896) xiv, p. 721, quoted in Eliade, *Patterns in Comparative Religion*, p. 246 (afterwards noted as Eliade, *Patterns*).
2. Mircea Eliade, *Myths, Dreams and Mysteries* (London: Harvill Press, 1960; London: Fontana Library, 1968) p. 157 Fontana edn (afterwards noted as Eliade, *Myths*).
3. Jacquetta Hawkes, *Man and the Sun* (London: The Cresset Press, 1962) pp. 60–1.
4. Rawson, *Primitive Erotic Art*, pp. 46–7.
5. Allegro, *Lost Gods*, p. 123.
6. Eliade, *Patterns*, pp. 259–60.
7. *Tales and Traditions of Tenby* (1858) p. 19.
8. Eliade, *Myths*, pp. 167–8.
9. Eliade, *Patterns*, p. 249.
10. A good modern study of Ice Age man is Evan Hadingham's *Secrets of the Ice Age* (London: William Heinemann, 1979).
11. Eliade, *Myths*, p. 171.
12. Rawson, op. cit., p. 40.
13. Eliade, *Myths*, pp. 172–3.
14. For worldwide examples from all periods, see Janet Bord, *Mazes and Labyrinths of the World* (London: Latimer New Dimensions, 1976).
15. Eliade, *Patterns*, p. 189.
16. Harold Bayley, *Archaic England* (London: Chapman & Hall, 1919) pp. 209, 717.
17. K. E. Maltwood, *A Guide to Glastonbury's Temple of the Stars* (London: James Clarke & Co. Ltd, 1964).
18. Geoffrey Ashe, *The Glastonbury Tor Maze* (Glastonbury: At the Foot of the Tree, 1979) p. 17.
19. Richard Williams, 'A History of the Parish of Llanbrynmair', *Collections Historical and Archaeological Relating to Montgomeryshire and its Borders* (London: Powysland Club, 1886) vol. XIX, p. 103.
20. Dames, *The Avebury Cycle*, chs 17 & 18; see also Aubrey Burl's criticism of this in his *Prehistoric Avebury* (London: Yale University Press, 1979) p. 142.

21. Dames, *The Silbury Treasure*.
22. In their book *The Wise Wound* (London: Victor Gollancz, 1978; London: Penguin Books, 1980) Penelope Shuttle and Peter Redgrove liken Silbury specifically to the cervix or birth-cone (p. 190 Penguin edn).
23. J. C. Cooper, *An Illustrated Encyclopaedia of Traditional Symbols* (London: Thames & Hudson, 1978) p. 37.
24. Frank Waters, *Book of the Hopi* (New York: Ballantine Books, 1969) pp. 154–61.
25. Rawson, op. cit., pp. 6–7; Leslie V. Grinsell, *Barrow, Pyramid and Tomb* (London: Thames & Hudson, 1975) ch. 2.
26. Joseph Campbell, *The Masks of God: Primitive Mythology* (London: Secker & Warburg, 1960) p. 67.
27. Eliade, *Patterns*, p. 252.
28. Neumann, *The Great Mother*, p. 159.
29. Campbell, op. cit., p. 447.
30. Dames, *The Silbury Treasure*, pp. 60–3.
31. *New Larousse Encyclopedia of Mythology* (London: Paul Hamlyn, 1959), and Robert Briffault (abridged by Gordon Rattray Taylor), *The Mothers* (London: George Allen & Unwin, 1959) ch. 23.
32. Ross, *Pagan Celtic Britain*, p. 297 Cardinal edn. For a fuller discussion of Celtic goddesses see pp. 265–97 of her book.
33. See Larousse, op. cit., p. 229; Ross, op. cit., pp. 281–6, 313.
34. Ross, op. cit., p. 290, also pp. 271, 453.
35. Fuller descriptions of the customs involving St Bride can be found in Donald A. Mackenzie, *Scottish Folk-Lore and Folk Life* (London and Glasgow: Blackie & Son, 1935) pp. 187–94, and Anne Ross, *The Folklore of the Scottish Highlands* (London: B. T. Batsford, 1976) pp. 125–31.
36. E. Estyn Evans, *Irish Folk Ways* (London: Routledge & Kegan Paul, 1957) pp. 211, 267–70.
37. Ross, *The Folklore of the Scottish Highlands*, p. 129.
38. Anne Ross, 'The Divine Hag of the Pagan Celts', in Venetia Newall, ed., *The Witch Figure* (London: Routledge & Kegan Paul, 1973) p. 156.
39. For many examples see John Michell, *Simulacra* (London: Thames & Hudson, 1979).

2 The Archaeological Evidence for Fertility Cults

1. See for example Aubrey Burl, *The Stone Circles of the British Isles* (London: Yale University Press, 1976) pp. 86–9.
2. Johannes Maringer, *The Gods of Prehistoric Man* (London: Weidenfeld & Nicolson, 1960) pp. 99, 195.
3. Neumann, *The Great Mother*, p. 96; the whole of ch. 9, 'The Primordial Goddess', deals with female figurines.
4. Evan Hadingham, *Secrets of the Ice Age* (London: William Heinemann, 1980) p. 225. This book is an excellent study of life in the Ice Age, and Hadingham deals specifically with the 'Venus figurines' on pp. 220–5. The opposite viewpoint is taken in the following books: Joseph Campbell,

The Masks of God: Primitive Mythology (London: Secker & Warburg, 1960) pp. 313–15, 324–30; G. R. Levy, *The Gate of Horn* (London: Faber & Faber, 1948) pp. 56–63; Maringer, op. cit., pp. 108–14.

5. James Dyer, *Southern England: An Archaeological Guide* (London: Faber & Faber, 1973) pp. 221–2.

6. On prehistoric fertility figures see Aubrey Burl, *Prehistoric Avebury* (London: Yale University Press, 1979) pp. 109–10, 221; Burl, *The Stone Circles of the British Isles*, op. cit., p. 88; Rawson, *Primitive Erotic Art*, p. 80.

7. Rawson, op. cit., pp. 81–2.

8. See P. V. Glob, *The Bog People* (London: Faber & Faber, 1969; London: Paladin Books, 1971).

9. Dyer, op. cit., pp. 81–2.

10. Both are illustrated side by side in Ross, *Pagan Celtic Britain*, p. 478 Cardinal edn.

11. ibid., p. 268.

12. For information on Brigantia see ibid., pp. 452–6.

13. ibid., pp. 138, 292.

14. Four excellent studies, mainly of the British carvings, are: Evan Hadingham, *Ancient Carvings in Britain* (London: Garnstone Press, 1974); Jean McMann, *Riddles of the Stone Age* (London: Thames & Hudson, 1980); Ronald W. B. Morris, *Prehistoric Rock Art of Argyll* (Poole: The Dolphin Press, 1977); Ronald W. B. Morris, *The Prehistoric Rock Art of Galloway and the Isle of Man* (Poole: Blandford Press, 1979).

15. London: Phoenix House, 1957.

16. See note 14 above.

17. In a letter to the authors.

18. Burl, *Prehistoric Avebury*, op. cit., pp. 221–5.

3 Fertility in Folklore

1. Leslie V. Grinsell, *Folklore of Prehistoric Sites in Britain* (Newton Abbot: David & Charles, 1976) p. 191.

2. ibid., pp. 187–9.

3. ibid., p. 207.

4. W. G. Wood-Martin, *Traces of the Elder Faiths of Ireland* (London: Longmans, Green & Co., 1902) vol. II, pp. 237–9.

5. Both from Janet and Colin Bord, *The Secret Country* (London: Paul Elek, 1976; London: Paladin Books, 1978) p. 54 Elek edn and pp. 47–8 Paladin edn.

6. Aubrey Burl, *Prehistoric Avebury* (London: Yale University Press, 1979) p. 216.

7. Grinsell, op. cit., p. 228.

8. Aubrey Burl, *The Stone Circles of the British Isles* (London: Yale University Press, 1976) p. 266.

9. Communication to the authors by a local resident.

10. For more details of the site and the legend, see Janet and Colin Bord, *A Guide to Ancient Sites in Britain* (London: Latimer New Dimensions, 1978; London: Paladin Books, 1979) pp. 70–1.

11. Listed, and the legends described, in S. P. Menefee, 'The "Merry Maidens" and the "Noce de Pierre"', *Folklore* vol. 85 (spring 1974) pp. 23–42.

12. Burl, *Prehistoric Avebury*, op. cit., p. 224.

13. Bord, *The Secret Country*, op. cit., p. 57 Elek edn.

14. Tony Deane and Tony Shaw, *The Folklore of Cornwall* (London: B. T. Batsford, 1975) p. 141.

15. Michael W. Burgess, *The Standing Stones of Norfolk and Suffolk*, East Suffolk and Norfolk Antiquarians Occasional Paper No. 1 (Lowestoft, 1978) p. 7.

16. Wood-Martin, op. cit., vol. II, p. 242.

17. J. M. McPherson, *Primitive Beliefs in the North-East of Scotland* (London: Longmans, Green & Co., 1929) p. 79.

18. Bord, *The Secret Country*, op. cit., p. 54.

19. Sir J. G. Frazer in *Folk-Lore* 29 (1918) p. 254.

20. Arthur Mitchell, *The Past in the Present* (Edinburgh: David Douglas, 1880) p. 265.

21. Wood-Martin, op. cit., vol. II, p. 247.

22. Anthony Weir, *Early Ireland, A Field Guide* (Belfast: Blackstaff Press, 1980) p. 113.

23. Wood-Martin, op. cit., vol. II, p. 242.

24. Bord, *The Secret Country*, op. cit., p. 56.

25. For worldwide examples see Eliade, *Patterns in Comparative Religion*, pp. 220–5; for further French examples see W. Branch Johnson, *Folktales of Brittany* (London: Methuen & Co., 1927) pp. 84–5.

26. Campbell Grant, *Rock Art of the American Indian* (New York: Promontory Press, 1967) p. 31.

27. Mircea Eliade, *A History of Religious Ideas*, vol. 1 – From the Stone Age to the Eleusinian Mysteries (London: Collins, 1979) pp. 116–18, 123.

28. Gooch, *Guardians of the Ancient Wisdom*, pp. 142–3, 149.

29. McPherson, op. cit., p. 79.

30. Bord, *The Secret Country*, op. cit., p. 54.

31. Wood-Martin, op. cit., vol. II, p. 28.

32. Quoted in ibid., vol. II, p. 29. On pages 28–9 are given other examples of saints' beds used for fertility purposes.

33. E. and M. A. Radford, edited and revised by Christina Hole, *Encyclopedia of Superstitions* (London: Hutchinson & Co., 1948, 1961) p. 51.

34. H. S. L. Dewar, *The Giant of Cerne Abbas*, West Country Folklore No. 1 ed. Theo Brown (Guernsey, C.I.: The Toucan Press, 1968).

35. *Folklore, Myths and Legends of Britain* (London: The Reader's Digest Association, 1973) p. 347.

36. ibid., p. 228.

37. Bord, *The Secret Country*, op. cit., pp. 54–5.

38. McPherson, op. cit., pp. 79–80.

39. Otta F. Swire, *The Outer Hebrides and Their Legends* (Edinburgh and London: Oliver & Boyd, 1966) pp. 101–2; Anne Ross, *The Folklore of the Scottish Highlands* (London: B. T. Batsford, 1976) pp. 148–50.

40. Radford and Hole, op. cit., p. 251.

41. ibid., p. 326.

42. Quoted in Wood-Martin, op. cit., vol. II, p. 233.

43. Bord, *The Secret Country*, op. cit., p. 55.

44. Peter Lancaster Brown, *Megaliths and Masterminds* (London: Robert Hale, 1979) p. 230.

45. The vernacular legend, taken from a history of Lincolnshire compiled *c.* 1850, is quoted in Ethel H. Rudkin, *Lincolnshire Folklore* (Gainsborough: Beltons, 1936; Wakefield: E. P. Publishing, 1973) pp. 69–70; see also Bord, *The Secret Country*, p. 57.

46. For examples of weather control through the ages, see D. Scott Rogo, 'Psychic Weather Control', *Fate* July 1980, pp. 79–85.

47. Marie Trevelyan, *Folk-Lore and Folk-Stories of Wales* (London: Elliot Stock, 1909; Wakefield: E. P. Publishing, 1973) p. 12.

48. J. Stevens Cox, *Prehistoric Monuments of Guernsey and Associated Folklore* (Guernsey, C.I.: The Toucan Press, 1976) pp. 27–8.

49. Bord, *The Secret Country*, op. cit., pp. 40–1.

50. ibid., p. 57.

51. ibid., pp. 57–8.

52. Eliade, *Patterns in Comparative Religion*, p. 219.

53. 'A Furness Diary', *The Countryman*, vol. LV no. 1 (spring 1958) p. 32.

54. Cox, op. cit., p. 12.

55. Bord, *The Secret Country*, op. cit., p. 39.

56. R. L. Tongue, *Somerset Folklore* (London: The Folklore Society, 1965) p. 166.

57. Michael Murphy, *At Slieve Gullion's Foot* (1940) p. 64, and E. Estyn Evans, *Irish Folk Ways* (London: Routledge & Kegan Paul, 1957) p. 103.

58. Bord, *The Secret Country*, op. cit., p. 57.

59. ibid., pp. 38–9.

60. Donald A. Mackenzie, *Scottish Folk-Lore and Folk Life* (London and Glasgow: Blackie & Son, 1935) p. 256.

61. Captain Thomas in *County Folk-Lore*, III (O.S.) p. 2, quoted in McPherson, op. cit., p. 81. Also see McPherson pp. 82–3 for possible late examples of stone worship.

62. Grinsell, op. cit., p. 253.

63. Hole, *British Folk Customs*, pp. 163–4.

64. Raoul Lemprière *Customs, Ceremonies and Traditions of the Channel Islands* (London: Robert Hale, 1976) pp. 171–2.

4 The Shapes of Standing Stones

1. (London: Frederick Muller, 1973) p. 56.

2. A. Thom, *Megalithic Sites in Britain* (Oxford: Oxford University Press, 1967) p. 68.

3. For discussion of the rebirth symbolism, see Eliade, *Patterns in Comparative Religion*, pp. 225–6.
4. Aubrey Burl, *Prehistoric Avebury* (London: Yale University Press, 1979) p. 70.
5. Harold Bayley, *Archaic England* (London: Chapman & Hall, 1919) p. 500.
6. Richard Rolt Brash, *The Ogam Inscribed Monuments of the Gaidhil* (London: Bell & Sons, 1879).
7. Thorkil Vanggaard, *Phallós* (London: Jonathan Cape, 1972) pp. 143–4.
8. For more information on these stones, see O. G. S. Crawford, *The Eye Goddess* (London: Phoenix House, 1957) p. 133.
9. Rawson, *Primitive Erotic Art*, pp. 78–9.
10. Barry Fell, *America B.C.* (New York: Quadrangle/The New York Times Book Co., 1976) ch. 14 'The Ritual Phallic Monuments'.
11. Charles J. Cazeau and Stuart D. Scott, Jr, *Exploring the Unknown* (New York: Plenum Press, 1979) pp. 52–60.
12. Rawson, op. cit., p. 43.
13. Anne Ross, 'Celtic and Northern Art', in Rawson, op. cit., p. 85.
14. The full story with associated legends is given in John Rhys, *Celtic Folklore, Welsh and Manx* (Oxford: Clarendon Press, 1901; London: Wildwood House, 1980) pp. 367–71.
15. J. Stevens Cox, *Prehistoric Monuments of Guernsey and Associated Folklore* (Guernsey, C.I.: Toucan Press, 1976) pp. 9–10.
16. Michael Harrison, *The Roots of Witchcraft* (London: Frederick Muller, 1973) p. 56.

5 Church Carvings: Sexual Themes, Green Men and Dragons

1. (London: Harvill Press, 1960; London: Fontana, 1968) pp. 186–7 Fontana edn.
2. Jørgen Andersen, *The Witch on the Wall*: Mediaeval Erotic Sculpture in the British Isles (London: George Allen & Unwin, 1977) pp. 22–3.
3. T. C. Lethbridge, *Witches*: Investigating an Ancient Religion (London: Routledge & Kegan Paul, 1962) pp. 87–8.
4. Michael Harrison, *The Roots of Witchcraft* (London: Frederick Muller, 1973) pp. 207–8.
5. G. R. Lewis, *Illustrations of Kilpeck* (London, 1842) p. 15, quoted in Andersen, op. cit., p. 10.
6. Anyone wishing to delve into this aspect is advised to read the two principal books on the subject, Jørgen Andersen's *The Witch on the Wall* and Anthony Weir's *Exhibitionism and the Iconography of Lust* (as yet unpublished).
7. Ronald Sheridan and Anne Ross, *Grotesques and Gargoyles* (Newton Abbot: David & Charles, 1975) pp. 18, 64.
8. Information from Anthony Weir in letters to the authors, and in his book *Exhibitionism and the Iconography of Lust* (as yet unpublished).
9. Anne Ross, 'The Divine Hag of the Pagan Celts' in Venetia Newall, ed., *The Witch Figure* (London: Routledge & Kegan Paul, 1973) p. 148; Rawson, *Primitive Erotic Art*, p. 104.

10. Information from Anthony Weir.
11. C. F. Tebbutt in a letter in *Folklore* vol. 84 (autumn 1973) pp. 254–5.
12. For example, in Harrison, op. cit., p. 206, and Brian Branston, *The Lost Gods of England* (London: Thames & Hudson, 1957, 1974) pp. 154–5.
13. *Chronicles of Lanercost*, noted in Margaret Murray, *The Witch-Cult in Western Europe* (Oxford: Oxford University Press, 1921) p. 23. That chapter, 'Continuity of the Religion', gives further evidence of continuing paganism.
14. Harrison, op. cit., p. 208.
15. ibid., pp. 209–10.
16. For examples see Rawson, op. cit., p. 75, and George Ryley Scott, *Phallic Worship* (London: Luxor Press, 1966; London: Panther Books, 1970) pp. 210–17 Panther edn.
17. Branston, op. cit., p. 200.
18. J. C. Cooper, *An Illustrated Encyclopaedia of Traditional Symbols* (London: Thames & Hudson, 1978) pp. 11, 103–4.
19. Scott, op. cit., pp. 220–1.
20. Quoted in Dames, *The Silbury Treasure*, p. 94.
21. E. O. James, *Origins of Sacrifice* (London: John Murray, 1933) p. 49.
22. Helen Hickey, *Images of Stone* (Belfast: Blackstaff Press, 1976) p. 57.
23. Eurwyn William, 'The Protection of the House: Some Iconographic Evidence from Wales', *Folklore*, vol. 89 (1978–II) pp. 148–53.
24. Theo Brown, *The Fate of the Dead* (Ipswich: D. S. Brewer, 1979) p. 12.
25. Mrs M. D. Anderson in a letter in *Folklore*, vol. 78 (winter 1967) pp. 306–7. Other 'tongue-pokers' are illustrated in Sheridan and Ross, op. cit., pp. 54–6.
26. Interested readers should consult Anthony Weir's comprehensive book *Exhibitionism and the Iconography of Lust* (as yet unpublished).
27. Dr Robert Plot, *The Natural History of Staffordshire* (1686); Jon Raven, *The Folklore of Staffordshire* (London: B. T. Batsford, 1978) p. 78.
28. Rawson, op. cit., p. 76.
29. Kathleen Basford, *The Green Man* (Ipswich: D. S. Brewer, 1978), which has a short, 21-page introductory text and 95 illustrations of carvings.
30. See her article 'The "Green Man" in Church Architecture', *Folk-Lore*, vol. 50 (1939) pp. 45–57.
31. G. B. Gardner, *The Meaning of Witchcraft* (Wellingborough: The Aquarian Press, 1959, 1971) p. 175.
32. Illustrated in Sheridan and Ross, op. cit., p. 32.
33. Basford, op. cit., p. 20.
34. ibid., p. 20.
35. For further discussion of the foliate head carvings, see R.O.M. and H. M. Carter, 'The Foliate Head in England', *Folklore*, vol. 78 (1967) pp. 269–74; Sheridan and Ross, op. cit., pp. 31–43; Roy Judge, *The Jack in the Green* (Ipswich: D. S. Brewer, 1979; Totowa, N. J.: Rowman & Littlefield, 1978) pp. 71–7.
36. Cooper, op. cit., p. 56.
37. J. E. Cirlot, *A Dictionary of Symbols* (London: Routledge & Kegan Paul, 1962) p. 87.

6 Holy Wells and Sacred Trees

1. Neumann, *The Great Mother*, pp. 48–9.
2. Celts of Hallstatt ancestry may have been in north-east Scotland around 600 BC – see Ross, *Pagan Celtic Britain*, p. 39 Cardinal edn.
3. ibid., pp. 51–4.
4. ibid., pp. 56, 280; Robert Charles Hope, *The Legendary Lore of the Holy Wells of England* (London: Elliot Stock, 1893; Detroit: Singing Tree Press, 1968) pp. 112–15.
5. A number of examples are given in Ross, op. cit., pp. 140–9.
6. Francis Jones, *The Holy Wells of Wales* (Cardiff: University of Wales Press, 1954) p. 38.
7. ibid., pp. 115–16.
8. *Folklore, Myths and Legends of Britain* (London: Reader's Digest Association, 1973) p. 175.
9. Charlotte S. Burne, ed., *Shropshire Folk-Lore* (London: Trübner & Co., 1883; Wakefield: E. P. Publishing, 1974) vol. 2, pp. 433–4.
10. Most books on customs and traditions include a description of well-dressing, but a comprehensive one is to be found in Christina Hole's *British Folk Customs*, pp. 212–14.
11. Marie Trevelyan, *Folk-Lore and Folk Stories of Wales* (first published London 1909; reissued Wakefield: E.P. Publishing, 1973) p. 14.
12. Burne, op. cit., pp. 417–18.
13. Ross, op. cit., pp. 230, 233.
14. W. G. Wood-Martin, *Traces of the Elder Faiths of Ireland* (London: Longmans, Green & Co., 1902) vol. II, p. 99. Other examples of Irish fertility wells can be found in Patrick Logan, *The Holy Wells of Ireland* (Gerrards Cross: Colin Smythe Ltd, 1980) pp. 81–2.
15. *Folklore, Myths and Legends of Britain*, op. cit., pp. 31, 448.
16. Antony D. Hippisley Coxe, *Haunted Britain* (London: Hutchinson & Co., 1973; London: Pan Books, 1975) p. 182 Pan edn.
17. J. M. McPherson, *Primitive Beliefs in the North-East of Scotland* (London: Longmans, Green & Co., 1929) p. 51.
18. W. Gregor, 'Guardian Spirits of Wells and Lochs', *Folk-Lore*, vol. 3 (1892) p. 68.
19. McPherson, op. cit., pp. 50–1, basing his account on the *Aberdeen Journal*, Notes and Queries, I, 68 (1908).
20. Jones, op. cit., pp. 99, 154, 155.
21. Hope, op. cit., pp. 107–8.
22. Enid Porter, *Cambridgeshire Customs and Folklore* (London: Routledge & Kegan Paul, 1969) p. 11.
23. Gentlemen's Magazine Library, iii, p. 389, quoted in Hope, op. cit., p. 122.
24. Kingsley Palmer, *Oral Folk-Tales of Wessex* (Newton Abbot: David & Charles, 1973) p. 76.
25. Coxe, op. cit., p. 26.
26. Tony Deane and Tony Shaw, *The Folklore of Cornwall* (London: B. T. Batsford, 1975) pp. 55, 159.

27. Wood-Martin, op. cit., pp. 86-7.
28. Vaughan Cornish, *Historic Thorn Trees in the British Isles* (London: Country Life, 1941) pp. 50, 54, 55, 57.
29. Wood Martin, op. cit., p. 156.
30. E. Estyn Evans, *Irish Folk Ways* (London: Routledge & Kegan Paul, 1957) p. 302.
31. Cornish, op. cit., p. 57.
32. Arthur Moore, *Manx Surnames and Place-Names*, p. 200.
33. Donald A. Mackenzie, *Scottish Folk-Lore and Folk Life* (London and Glasgow: Blackie & Son, 1935) p. 268.
34. Ross, op. Cit., pp. 54-5.
35. E. and M. A. Radford, ed. and rev. by Christina Hole, *Encyclopedia of Superstitions* (London: Hutchinson & Co., 1961) pp. 185-6.
36. R. C. Skyring Walters, *The Ancient Wells, Springs, and Holy Wells of Gloucestershire* (Bristol: The St Stephen's Press, 1928) p. 53.
37. Mackenzie, op. cit., p. 269.
38. Walters, op. cit., p. 23.
39. ibid., p. 25.
40. G. H. Doble, *Saint Melor: A Cornish Saint* (Shipston-on-Stour, 1927) p. 7, quoted in Ross, op. cit., pp. 144-5.
41. Eliade, *Patterns in Comparative Religion,* pp. 266-7. The whole of Chapter VIII, 'Vegetation: Rites and Symbols of Regeneration', deals in depth with the cults around the world.
42. For example, J. H. Wilks, *Trees of the British Isles in History and Legend* (London: Frederick Muller, 1972).
43. Marjorie Rowling, *The Folklore of the Lake District* (London: B. T. Batsford, 1976) p. 96.
44. For more information on the cult, see Cornish, op. cit., ch. IV, and D. A. MacManus, *The Middle Kingdom* (London: Max Parrish, 1959; Gerrards Cross: Colin Smythe, 1972) ch. 3.
45. For more information on the Holy Thorn, see Cornish, op. cit., ch. VI; A. R. Vickery, 'Holy Thorn of Glastonbury', West Country Folklore monograph No. 12 (Guernsey, C. I.: Toucan Press, 1979).
46. Wendy Boase, *The Folklore of Hampshire and the Isle of Wight* (London: B. T. Batsford, 1976) p. 118.
47. Hole, *British Folk Customs*, p. 26.
48. For more information, see ibid., pp. 147-8. In *The Folklore of Wiltshire* (London: B. T. Batsford, 1976, pp. 36-9) Ralph Whitlock describes how he took part in the Wishford celebrations 'a few years ago'.
49. Hole, op. cit., pp. 22-3; Homer Sykes, *Once a Year* (London: Gordon Fraser, 1977) p. 71.
50. Ralph Whitlock, *The Folklore of Devon* (London: B. T. Batsford, 1977) p. 173.
51. Trefor M. Owen, *Welsh Folk Customs* (Cardiff: National Museum of Wales, 1968) p. 110.
52. For a history of the Christmas tree, see Hole, op. cit., pp. 53-4.
53. Neumann, op. cit., p. 49.
54. ibid., pp. 48-9.

55. Allegro, *Lost Gods*, p. 129.
56. Radford and Hole, op. cit., p. 185.
57. Eliade, op. cit., pp. 287-8.
58. ibid., p. 292.
59. Neumann, op. cit., p. 252.
60. For a wider study, see Frazer, *The Golden Bough*, ch. IX 'The Worship of Trees', ch. X 'Relics of Tree-Worship in Modern Europe', ch. XV 'The Worship of the Oak', and ch. XXVIII 'The Killing of the Tree-Spirit'.
61. The custom is recorded by Dr Frank Elgee, writing in Cornish, op. cit., p. 30.
62. Wilks, op. cit., p. 202.
63. Boase, op. cit., pp. 117-18.
64. Radford and Hole, op. cit., p. 254.
65. Robert Graves, *The White Goddess* (London: Faber & Faber, paperback edition 1961) p. 125.
66. ibid., p. 125; Radford and Hole, op. cit., pp. 233-5.
67. Frazer, op. cit., ch. LXV.
68. Radford and Hole, op. cit., p. 253.
69. S. O. Addy, *Household Tales, with Other Traditional Remains collected in the Counties of York, Lincoln, Derby and Nottingham* (1895), quoted in Radford and Hole, op. cit., p. 242.
70. L. Rider Haggard, *I Walk at Night* (1935), quoted in Radford and Hole, op. cit., p. 256.
71. Radford and Hole, op. cit., p. 251.
72. R. L. Tongue, *Somerset Folklore* (London: Folk-Lore Society, 1965) p. 31.
73. Wilks, op. cit., p. 131.
74. Frazer, op. cit., pp. 156-7.
75. ibid., pp. 156-8, 163-4.
76. Eliade, op. cit., p. 309.

7 The Agricultural Cycle: Preparing the Ground

1. Neumann, *The Great Mother*, p. 52.
2. *Proceedings of the Linnean Society of New South Wales*, vol. viii, pp. 436-7 (21 February 1884), reprinted in *The Folk-Lore Journal*, vol. II part VII (July 1884) pp. 220-1.
3. Indianapolis, Indiana, *Star*, 24 February 1981, quoting from the Shanghai *Liberation Daily*.
4. E. and M. A. Radford, ed. and rev. by Christina Hole, *The Encyclopaedia of Superstitions* (London: Hutchinson & Co., 1961) p. 278.
5. ibid., p. 278.
6. Quoted in Frederick Ernest Sawyer, F.M.S., 'S. Swithin and Rainmakers', *The Folk-Lore Journal*, vol. I part VII (July 1883) p. 214, which article also contains information on rain-making rituals worldwide.
7. Other similar beliefs are given in Radford and Hole, op. cit., p. 277.
8. E. Estyn Evans, *Irish Folk Ways* (London: Routledge & Kegan Paul, 1957) pp. 100-1.

9. Donald A. MacKenzie, *Scottish Folk-Lore and Folk Life* (London and Glasgow: Blackie & Son, 1935) p. 253.

10. Eve Blantyre Simpson, *Folk Lore in Lowland Scotland* (first published 1908; reissued Wakefield: E.P. Publishing, 1976) p. 124.

11. John Gregorson Campbell, *Witchcraft and Second Sight in the Highlands and Islands of Scotland* (first published 1902; reissued Wakefield: E. P. Publishing, 1974) pp. 261–2.

12. Walter Gregor, 'Some Old Farming Customs and Notions in Aberdeenshire', *The Folk-Lore Journal*, vol. II part XI (Nov. 1884) p. 331.

13. Recorded in the diary of Nicholas Blundell and quoted in Hole, *British Folk Customs*, p. 126.

14. (No author given), *A World of Stone*: Life, Folklore and Legends of the Aran Islands (Dublin: O'Brien Educational, n.d.) p. 97.

15. Geoffrey Hoyland, 'The Holy Mountain of Gwent', *The Countryman*, vol. LIV no. 3 (autumn 1957) p. 469.

16. *A World of Stone*, op. cit., p. 97.

17. Alasdair Alpin MacGregor, *The Peat-Fire Flame* (Edinburgh and London: The Moray Press, 1937) p. 65.

18. MacKenzie, op. cit., p. 244; Katharine M. Briggs, *The Vanishing People* (London: B. T. Batsford, 1978) p. 156.

19. Marie Trevelyan, *Folk-Lore and Folk-Stories of Wales* (London, 1909; Wakefield: E. P. Publishing, 1973) p. 263.

20. MacKenzie, op. cit., p. 80.

21. McLean, *The Four Fire Festivals*, pp. 5–7.

22. *Gentleman's Magazine*, February 1795, quoted in John Harland and T. T. Wilkinson, *Lancashire Folk-Lore* (first published 1882; reissued Wakefield: E. P. Publishing, 1973) p. 47.

23. Trevelyan, op. cit., pp. 27–8.

24. Frazer, *The Golden Bough*, pp. 814–28, 845.

25. Anne Ross, *The Folklore of the Scottish Highlands* (London: B. T. Batsford, 1976) p. 153.

26. Rawson, *Primitive Erotic Art*, p. 76.

27. J. M. McPherson, *Primitive Beliefs in the North-East of Scotland* (London: Longmans, Green & Co., 1929) p. 6.

28. Ernest W. Marwick, *The Folklore of Orkney and Shetland* (London: B. T. Batsford, 1975) p. 112.

29. Ross, op. cit., pp. 135–6.

30. A. W. Moore, *The Folk-Lore of the Isle of Man* (first published 1891; reissued Wakefield: S. R. Publishers, 1971) pp. 110, 118.

31. Frazer, op. cit., p. 826.

32. Alan Gailey, 'The Bonfire in North Irish Tradition', *Folklore*, vol. 88, I (1977) p. 15.

33. *A World of Stone*, op. cit., p. 97.

34. Charlotte Elizabeth, *Personal Recollections*, quoted from 'S.M.', *Sketches of Irish History* (1845), quoted in Harold Bayley, *Archaic England* (London: Chapman & Hall, 1919) pp. 803–4, fn 3.

35. Ella Mary Leather, *The Folk-Lore of Herefordshire* (first published 1912; reissued Wakefield: S. R. Publishers, 1970) pp. 93–4; Jacqueline

Simpson, *The Folklore of the Welsh Border* (London: B. T. Batsford, 1976) pp. 135–6; Hole, *British Folk Customs*, pp. 197–8.

36. Leather, op. cit., pp. 91–3.
37. Hole, op. cit., p. 36.
38. Frazer, op. cit., ch. LXII.
39. Evans, op. cit., p. 148.
40. This custom is described in Chapter 10.
41. Trefor M. Owen, *Welsh Folk Customs* (Cardiff: National Museum of Wales, 1968) p. 48.
42. Homer Sykes, *Once a Year* (London: Gordon Fraser, 1977) pp. 18–19.
43. ibid., p. 157.
44. Hole, op. cit., p. 39.
45. This example, and others, are given in 'Human sacrifice for the crops' in E. O. James, *Origins of Sacrifice* (London: John Murray, 1933) pp. 96–100. For further discussion on the importance of sacrifice, see Eliade, *Patterns in Comparative Religion*, pp. 341–7.
46. *Folklore, Myths and Legends of Britain* (London: The Reader's Digest Association, 1973) p. 312.
47. Aubrey Burl, *Prehistoric Avebury* (London: Yale University Press, 1979) pp. 99, 213.
48. James, op. cit., p. 34.
49. A report in the *Manx Sun* newspaper in 1853, quoted in Moore, op. cit., p. 93. More information on the Isle of Man rituals is given in John Rhys, *Celtic Folklore: Welsh and Manx* (Oxford: Clarendon Press, 1901; London: Wildwood House, 1980) vol. I, pp. 306–8.
50. J. L. Campbell, ed., *A Collection of Highland Rites and Customes* (Ipswich: D. S. Brewer, 1975) p. 63.
51. See A. W. Smith, 'The Luck in the Head: A Problem in English Folklore', *Folklore*, vol. 73 (spring 1962) pp. 13–24.
52. Rawson, op. cit., pp. 50, 74.
53. For more information on the Haxey Hood Game, see Hole, op. cit., pp. 94–7.
54. W. G. Wood-Martin, *Traces of the Elder Faiths of Ireland* (London: Longmans, Green & Co., 1902) vol. II, p. 6.
55. Hole, op. cit., pp. 29–30.
56. Ruth E. St Leger-Gordon, *The Witchcraft and Folklore of Dartmoor* (London: Robert Hale, 1965; Wakefield: E. P. Publishing, 1973) p. 150.
57. *East Anglian Daily Times*, 15 April 1965.
58. Gregor, op. cit., pp. 329–30.
59. McPherson, op. cit., pp. 86–9.
60. H. R. Ellis Davidson, *Gods and Myths of Northern Europe* (Harmondsworth: Penguin Books, 1964) p. 114.
61. Neumann, *The Great Mother*, p. 303 fn. 51.
62. P. V. Glob, *The Mound People* (London, 1974) pp. 149–50.
63. The Swedish source of their information is noted by Peter Gelling and Hilda Ellis Davidson, who note the custom in their *The Chariot of the Sun* (London: J. M. Dent & Sons, 1969) p. 79.

64. Geoffrey Palmer and Noel Lloyd, *A Year of Festivals* (London: Frederick Warne & Co., 1972) p. 100; Hole, op. cit., pp. 157–8.

8 The Agricultural Cycle: From Seed-time to Harvest

1. (London: Faber & Faber, 1966) p. 127.
2. Frazer, *The Golden Bough*, pp. 423–4.
3. Roy Palmer, *The Folklore of Warwickshire* (London: B. T. Batsford, 1976) p. 62.
4. Frazer, op. cit., p. 868.
5. The words of Mircea Eliade in his *Patterns in Comparative Religion*, p. 355; see also Frazer, op. cit., pp. 178–83, and Rawson, *Primitive Erotic Art*, p. 52.
6. Eliade, op. cit., p. 355.
7. Frazer, op. cit., p. 422.
8. Hole, *British Folk Customs*, p. 186.
9. Charlotte S. Burne, ed., *Shropshire Folk-Lore* (first published 1883; reissued Wakefield: E. P. Publishing, 1974) vol. 2 p. 338.
10. *Yorkshire Gazette*, 7 April 1883, quoted in *The Folk-Lore Journal*, vol. 1, part VIII (August 1883) pp. 269–70.
11. Ella Mary Leather, *The Folk-Lore of Herefordshire* (first published 1912; reissued Wakefield: S. R. Publishers, 1970) p. 100. More information on heaving can be found in: Hole, op. cit., pp. 68–70; Burne, op. cit., pp. 336–40; Trefor M. Owen, *Welsh Folk Customs* (Cardiff: National Museum of Wales, 1968) pp. 89–91.
12. Hole, op. cit., pp. 167–8.
13. Leather, op. cit., p. 99.
14. ibid., p. 99.
15. Jacqueline Simpson, *The Folklore of the Welsh Border* (London: B. T. Batsford, 1976) p. 147.
16. Leather, op. cit., p. 100.
17. *Folk-Lore*, vol. XXII (1911), quoted in Katharine M. Briggs, *The Folklore of the Cotswolds* (London: B. T. Batsford, 1974) p. 40.
18. Details of local wassailing customs can be found in most books of folklore covering the areas where the custom was prevalent, i.e. Cornwall, Devon, Somerset, Kent, Sussex, Gloucestershire, Worcestershire, Herefordshire, Wiltshire and Gwent, but a good general summary appears in Hole, op. cit., pp. 209–10.
19. Thomas Pennant, *A Tour in Scotland* (Warrington, 1769).
20. R. L. Tongue, ed. K. M. Briggs, *Somerset Folklore* (London: The Folk-Lore Society, 1965) p. 149.
21. Hole, op. cit., p. 77; Homer Sykes, *Once a Year* (London: Gordon Fraser, 1977) p. 66.
22. The richness of harvest customs around the world, and comparisons with British customs, are shown in Frazer's *The Golden Bough*, where four chapters are especially relevant: XLV 'The Corn-Mother and the Corn-Maiden in Northern Europe', XLVI 'The Corn-Mother in Many Lands', XLVII 'Lityerses', and XLVIII 'The Corn-Spirit as an Animal'.

23. Quoted in Anne Ross, *The Folklore of the Scottish Highlands* (London: B. T. Batsford, 1976) p. 139.
24. Quoted in ibid., pp. 139–40.
25. Hole, op. cit., p. 119.
26. Margaret Killip, *The Folklore of the Isle of Man* (London: B. T. Batsford, 1975) p. 176.
27. Owen, op. cit., p. 114.
28. Leather, op. cit., p. 104.
29. Frazer, op. cit., ch. XLVIII, especially pp. 607–8.
30. Ross, op. cit., pp. 143–4; Frazer, op. cit., pp. 530–1.
31. Enid Porter, *Cambridgeshire Customs and Folklore* (London: Routledge & Kegan Paul, 1969) pp. 120–1.
32. Owen, op. cit., p. 117.
33. A. W. Moore, *The Folk-Lore of the Isle of Man* (first published 1891; reissued Wakefield: S. R. Publishers, 1971) p. 122.
34. Both Llansilin examples from Owen, op. cit., p. 118, the quote being from *Bye-gones*, 31 October 1928.
35. Kingsley Palmer, *The Folklore of Somerset* (London: B. T. Batsford, 1976) p. 104.
36. Ralph Whitlock, *The Folklore of Devon* (London: B. T. Batsford, 1977) p. 151.
37. Tongue, op. cit., p. 168.
38. Whitlock, op. cit., p. 151.
39. Sarah Hewett, *Nummits and Crummits* (first published 1900; Reissued Wakefield: E.P. Publishing, 1976) p. 98.
40. Ross, op. cit., p. 143; Frazer, op. cit., p. 537.
41. Owen, op. cit., pp. 119–20.
42. All these and more are described and illustrated in M. Lambeth, *A Golden Dolly* (London: John Baker, 1969), which also shows how to make dollies.
43. Naomi Mitchison, 'A Harvest Experience', *Folklore*, vol. 84 (autumn 1973) pp. 252–3.
44. Celia Gardner, 'Symbols of Life', *The Countryman*, vol. 65 no. 2 (winter 1965) p. 274. She also describes how after the hay harvest a farmer left a tiny 'doll' fastened to a tree stem.
45. Hole, op. cit., p. 94.

9   The Ritual Sacrifice of the Divine Victim

1. (London: John Murray, 1933) p. 33.
2. Frazer, *The Golden Bough*, ch. XXIV.
3. ibid., ch. VI.
4. ibid., p. 117.
5. Hugh Ross Williamson, *The Arrow and the Sword* (London: Faber & Faber, 1947) p. 23.
6. For a full discussion of sacrifice, see E. O. James, *Origins of Sacrifice* (London: John Murray, 1933).
7. J. C. Cooper, *An Illustrated Encyclopaedia of Traditional Symbols*

(London: Thames & Hudson, 1978) pp. 117–18; J. E. Cirlot, *A Dictionary of Symbols* (London: Routledge & Kegan Paul, 1962) p. 233.

8. Examples of dismemberment and blood sprinkling are given in Margaret Murray, *The Divine King in England* (London: Faber & Faber, 1954) pp. 35–9.
9. See the Introduction in ibid., pp. 13–18.
10. In the latter see ch. VI 'The Divine Victim' (London: Sampson Low, Marston & Co., n.d.).
11. See Murray, *The Divine King in England*, op. cit.
12. The account of William Rufus's death was compiled from Margaret Murray's two books *The God of the Witches* and *The Divine King in England*.
13. Margaret Murray's version of Becket's death is given in *The God of the Witches*, pp. 168–74; see also Donald Attwater, *The Penguin Dictionary of Saints* (Harmondsworth: Penguin Books, 1965) pp. 325–6.
14. Joan of Arc's story is told in Régine Pernoud, *Joan of Arc* (London: Evergreen Books, 1961), and briefly in Attwater, op. cit., p. 187.
15. Murray, *The God of the Witches*, op. cit., p. 176.
16. Geoffrey Palmer and Noel Lloyd, *A Year of Festivals* (London: Frederick Warne & Co., 1972) pp. 21–2.
17. Hole, *British Folk Customs*, pp. 94–7.
18. ibid., pp. 97–100.
19. J. M. McPherson, *Primitive Beliefs in the North-East of Scotland* (London: Longmans, Green & Co., 1929) p. 9.
20. Hole, op. cit., pp. 164, 165.
21. McPherson, op. cit., pp. 34–6.
22. Homer Sykes, *Once a Year* (London: Gordon Fraser, 1977) p. 114; Hole, op. cit., p. 39; and for general worldwide practices see Frazer, op. cit., pp. 746–56.
23. See, for example, E. O. James, *Origins of Sacrifice* (London: John Murray, 1933).

10 Traditional Customs with Fertility Overtones: Banishing Winter and Welcoming Spring

1. McLean, *The Four Fire Festivals*, p. 29.
2. Frazer, *The Golden Bough*, pp. 831, 832; Hole, *British Folk Customs*, p. 88.
3. Frazer, op. cit., p. 830.
4. Hole, op. cit., pp. 87, 89; McLean, op. cit., p. 15; Anne Ross, *The Folklore of the Scottish Highlands* (London: B. T. Batsford, 1976) p. 153.
5. Frazer, op. cit., p. 831.
6. ibid., p. 832; Hole, op. cit., p. 88.
7. Hole, op. cit., p. 88.
8. For more information see ibid., p. 84, and McLean, op. cit., p. 15.
9. Information on the Yule log is given in the following sources: Hole, op. cit., pp. 220–2, 223; E. O. James, *Origins of Sacrifice* (London: John Murray, 1933) p. 55; Frazer, op. cit., pp. 833–5; E. and M. A. Radford,

ed. and rev. by Christina Hole, *The Encyclopaedia of Superstitions* (London: Hutchinson & Co., 1948, 1961) p. 23; McLean, op. cit.

10. Homer Sykes, *Once a Year* (London: Gordon Fraser, 1977) pp. 150, 154; Geoffrey Palmer and Noel Lloyd, *A Year of Festivals* (London: Frederick Warne & Co., 1972) p. 93; Radford and Hole, op. cit., pp. 23–4; Frazer, op. cit., p. 833.

11. Eliade, *Patterns in Comparative Religion*, p. 415.

12. Ernest W. Marwick, *The Folklore of Orkney and Shetland* (London: B. T. Batsford, 1975) p. 69.

13. Hole, op. cit., p. 150.

14. John Harland and T. T. Wilkinson, *Lancashire Folk-Lore* (first published 1882; reissued Wakefield: S. R. Publishers, 1972, E. P. Publishing, 1973) p. 231.

15. Hole, op. cit., p. 150; Palmer and Lloyd, op. cit., p. 137.

16. Jacqueline Simpson, *The Folklore of the Welsh Border* (London: B. T. Batsford, 1976) p. 144.

17. Hole, op. cit., pp. 62–3.

18. *Daily Chronicle*, 4 April 1919, quoted in Harold Bayley, *Archaic England* (London: Chapman & Hall, 1919) p. 756 fn. 2.

19. Palmer and Lloyd, op. cit., p. 140; Hole, op. cit., pp. 65, 66; Ethel H. Rudkin, *Lincolnshire Folklore* (first published 1936; reissued Wakefield: E. P. Publishing, 1973) p. 45.

20. *Bye-gones*, 19 October 1892, quoted in Trefor M. Owen, *Welsh Folk Customs* (Cardiff: National Museum of Wales, 1968) p. 87 fn. 2.

21. Simpson, op. cit., p. 146.

22. Frazer, op. cit., p. 159; Hole, op. cit., p. 136.

23. Eliade, op. cit., pp. 354–8.

24. Present-day examples of this kind of effect are shown in the spoon-bending phenomenon (see for example John Taylor, *Superminds*: An Investigation into the Paranormal (London: Macmillan, 1975; London: Picador Books, 1976)), in the intentional production of a 'ghost' in Toronto in the 1970s (Iris M. Owen with Margaret Sparrow, *Conjuring up Philip* (Ontario: Fitzhenry & Whiteside, 1976; PaperJacks, 1977)), and in the performances of poltergeists (Alan Gauld and A. D. Cornell, *Poltergeists* (London: Routledge & Kegan Paul, 1979)).

25. William Andrews, ed., *Historic Byways and Highways of Old England* (London: William Andrews & Co., 1900) p. 95.

26. Hole, op. cit., p. 137.

27. Phillip Stubbes, *Anatomie of Abuses* (London, 1583), quoted in Frazer, op. cit., p. 162.

28. Andrews, op. cit., p. 98.

29. Hole, op. cit., p. 137; Palmer and Lloyd, op. cit., p. 17.

30. Hole, op. cit., p. 128.

31. Frazer, op. cit., pp. 158–68.

32. Eliade, op. cit., p. 313.

33. ibid., p. 314.

34. Hole, op. cit., p. 136.

35. Simpson, op. cit., p. 150.
36. Christina Hole, *Traditions and Customs of Cheshire* (London: Williams & Norgate, 1937; reissued Wakefield: S. R. Publishers, 1970) p. 88.
37. Palmer and Lloyd, op. cit., p. 19.
38. Sykes, op. cit., pp. 58, 80.
39. Eliade, op. cit., p. 358.
40. Frazer, op. cit., p. 159.
41. J. Donaldson, *Upper Fews in 1838*, p. 70, quoted in E. Estyn Evans, *Irish Folk Ways* (London: Routledge & Kegan Paul, 1957) p. 273.
42. A. W. Moore, *The Folk-Lore of the Isle of Man* (first published 1891; reissued Wakefield: S. R. Publishers, 1971) p. 112; Hole, *British Folk Customs*, p. 135.
43. Frazer, op. cit., pp. 416–17.
44. Eliade, op. cit., p. 320.
45. Wirt Sikes, *British Goblins* (London: Sampson Low, 1880; reissued Wakefield: E. P. Publishing, 1973) p. 276.
46. Roy Judge, *The Jack-in-the-Green* (Ipswich: D. S. Brewer, 1979; Totowa, N. J.: Rowman & Littlefield, 1978) p. 73.
47. ibid., p. 73.
48. Frazer, op. cit., pp. 166–7.
49. Judge, op. cit., p. xi.
50. ibid., pp. 18–20.
51. ibid., pp. 3–5.
52. Frazer, op. cit., pp. 835, 838–9.
53. Judge, op. cit., pp. 28–9.
54. ibid., pp. 41–5.
55. Palmer and Lloyd, op. cit., p. 32; Sykes, op. cit., p. 74.

11 Traditional Customs with Fertility Overtones: Water, Sun, Horses, Horns and She-Males

1. (London: Harvill Press, 1960; London: Fontana Books, 1968) p. 189 Fontana edn.
2. Eliade, *Patterns in Comparative Religion*, pp. 188–90.
3. Hole, *British Folk Customs*, pp. 145–6.
4. Trefor M. Owen, *Welsh Folk Customs* (Cardiff: National Museum of Wales, 1968) pp. 43, 68.
5. Tony Deane and Tony Shaw, *The Folklore of Cornwall* (London: B. T. Batsford, 1975) p. 170; Hole, op. cit., p. 134; Violet Alford, *The Hobby Horse and Other Animal Masks* (London: Merlin Press, 1975) p. 42.
6. Hole, op. cit., p. 65.
7. W. G. Wood-Martin, *Traces of the Elder Faiths of Ireland* (London: Longmans, Green, & Co., 1902) p. 265.
8. Jacqueline Simpson, *The Folklore of the Welsh Border* (London: B. T. Batsford, 1976) pp. 138–9; Charlotte S. Burne, ed., *Shropshire Folk-Lore* (London: Trübner & Co., 1883; Wakefield: E. P. Publishing, 1973) vol. 2, pp. 320–1; Frederick Ernest Sawyer, 'S. Swithin and Rainmakers', *The Folk-Lore Journal*, vol. I part VII (July 1883) p. 214.

9. Frazer, *The Golden Bough*, pp. 417–18.
10. Owen, op. cit., p. 45.
11. Wirt Sikes, *British Goblins* (London: Sampson Low, 1880; Wakefield: E. P. Publishing, 1973) p. 254.
12. Geoffrey Palmer and Noel Lloyd, *A Year of Festivals* (London: Frederick Warne & Co., 1972) p. 137.
13. Ralph Whitlock, *The Folklore of Wiltshire* (London: B. T. Batsford, 1976), p. 52.
14. Hole, op. cit., p. 149.
15. Homer Sykes, *Once a Year* (London: Gordon Fraser, 1977) p. 85.
16. Hole, op. cit., p. 46.
17. Burne, op. cit., vol. 2, p. 33; Hole, op. cit., p. 152.
18. Whitlock, op. cit., pp. 23, 53.
19. Hole, op. cit., pp. 71, 189.
20. J. C. Cooper, *An Illustrated Encyclopaedia of Traditional Symbols* (London: Thames & Hudson, 1978) p. 66.
21. Evan Hadingham, *Secrets of the Ice Age* (London: William Heinemann, 1979) p. 182.
22. Ross, *Pagan Celtic Britain*, pp. 172–94, 404–17, Cardinal edn.
23. E. C. Cawte, *Ritual Animal Disguise* (Ipswich: D. S. Brewer, 1978; Totowa, N. J.: Rowman & Littlefield, 1978) pp. 85–93; Hole, op. cit., p. 100.
24. Cawte, op. cit., pp. 125–7; Hole, op. cit., pp. 187–8; Sykes, op. cit., p. 144.
25. Frazer, op. cit., p. 836.
26. Cawte, op. cit., p. 100.
27. Owen, op. cit., pp. 50–6; Cawte, op. cit., pp. 94–102; Hole, op. cit., p. 124.
28. Hole, op. cit., p. 112; Cawte, op. cit., pp. 153–6; Wood-Martin, op. cit., p. 268.
29. Tony Deane and Tony Shaw, *The Folklore of Cornwall* (London: B. T. Batsford, 1975) p. 168.
30. ibid., p. 169.
31. ibid., p. 169.
32. ibid., pp. 168–70; Cawte, op. cit., pp. 157–62; Hole, op. cit., pp. 133–4.
33. Vince Russett, 'Minehead's May Celebrations', *Picwinnard* 4 (April 1978) pp. 3–10; Cawte, op. cit., pp. 168–74; Hole, op. cit., p. 134.
34. Cawte, op. cit., pp. 65–76; Hole, op. cit., p. 103.
35. Hole, op. cit., p. 47; Cawte, op. cit., pp. 142–4.
36. Hole, op. cit., pp. 207–8.
37. Cawte, op. cit., p. 117.
38. ibid., p. 153; *Folklore, Myths and Legends of Britain* (London: Reader's Digest Association, 1973) p. 164; Margaret Murray, *The God of the Witches* (London: Sampson Low, Marston & Co., n.d.) p. 31.
39. Hole, op. cit., p. 105; Palmer and Lloyd, op. cit., p. 167.
40. Hole, op. cit., p. 163.
41. Ross, op. cit., pp. 410, 405.
42. Wood-Martin, op. cit., p. 268.
43. Ross, op. cit., pp. 180, 202–9, 213.

44. Attributed to Theodore, a sixth-century Archbishop of Canterbury, but probably from a ninth-century Frankish document. See Hole, op. cit., p. 47.
45. Sykes, op. cit., p. 80.
46. Cawte, op. cit., p. 224.
47. Attributed to Severian, and quoted in Cawte, op. cit., p. 225.
48. Owen, op. cit., p. 105.

12 Earth Energies and the Maintenance of Fertility

1. Adam McLean, 'The Alchemy of the Earth Forces', *The Hermetic Journal*, No. 10 (winter 1980) p. 17.
2. Alfred Watkins, *The Old Straight Track*: Its Mounds, Beacons, Moats, Sites and Mark Stones (London: Methuen & Co., 1925; London: Garnstone Press, 1970; London: Abacus Books, 1974).
3. (London: Garnstone Press, 1969; London: Abacus Books, 1973).
4. ibid., p. 71 Garnstone edn.
5. For more detailed information, read Paul Screeton, *Quicksilver Heritage* (Wellingborough: Thorsons Publishers, 1974; London: Abacus Books, 1976) and Paul Devereux and Ian Thomson, *The Ley Hunter's Companion* (London: Thames & Hudson, 1979); and for the continuing story subscribe to *The Ley Hunter* magazine (P.O. Box 13, Welshpool, Powys) and *Northern Earth Mysteries* (15 Convent Court, Park Grove, Hull, HU5 2UJ).
6. Hole, *British Folk Customs*, p. 181.
7. ibid., p. 64.
8. ibid., pp. 67–8.
9. ibid., pp. 216–17.
10. Eliade, *Patterns in Comparative Religion*, p. 320.
11. Marjorie Rowling, *The Folklore of the Lake District* (London: B. T. Batsford, 1976) p. 119.
12. Janet and Colin Bord, *The Secret Country* (London: Paul Elek, 1976; London: Paladin Books, 1978) p. 22 Elek edn.
13. Hole, op. cit., p. 186.
14. ibid., pp. 186–7.
15. Bord, op. cit., pp. 23–4.
16. J. Stevens Cox, *Prehistoric Monuments of Guernsey and Associated Folklore* (Guernsey, C.I.: Toucan Press, 1976) p. 26.
17. Bord, op. cit., p. 23.
18. H. S. L. Dewar, *The Giant of Cerne Abbas*, West Country Folklore monograph No. 1 (Guernsey, C.I.: Toucan Press, 1968) p. 8.
19. Kathleen Wiltshire, *Wiltshire Folklore* (Salisbury: Compton Russell, 1975) p. 107.
20. Bord, op. cit., p. 22.
21. Ralph Whitlock, *The Folklore of Wiltshire* (London: B. T. Batsford, 1976) pp. 28, 52.
22. Bord, op. cit., p. 24.

23. E. Estyn Evans, *Irish Folk Ways* (London: Routledge & Kegan Paul, 1957) p. 276.

24. Jeremy Harte, 'Old Games and Rituals', *The Ley Hunter*, no. 82 (1978) pp. 3–6.

25. For examples of its use, see Tom Graves, ed., *Dowsing and Archaeology* (Wellingborough: Turnstone Press, 1980), an anthology of articles from the *Journal* of the British Society of Dowsers.

26. Guy Underwood, *The Pattern of the Past* (London: Pitman Publishing, 1969; London: Abacus Books, 1972).

27. ibid., p. 39 Pitman edn.

28. ibid., ch. 6.

29. Devereux and Thomson, op. cit., p. 140.

30. Graves, *Needles of Stone*, p. 17 Turnstone edn; see ch. 2 for a discussion of Underwood's work.

31. ibid., pp. 34–8.

32. ibid., p. 49.

33. Tom Graves, 'Leys and Dowsing', *The Ley Hunter*, no. 77 (1977) pp. 3–4.

34. Graves, *Needles of Stone*, pp. 59–64.

35. ibid., p. 68.

36. ibid., p. 69.

37. ibid., p. 117.

38. For further details see the reports published in *The Ley Hunter:* Dr G. V. Robins, 'The Dragon Awakes', in no. 87 (1979/80) pp. 3–7; Paul Devereux, 'Operation Merlin', in no. 88 (spring 1980) pp. 16–19; Paul Devereux, 'Operation Merlin 2', in no. 89 (summer/autumn 1980) pp. 25–6.

39. Robins, op. cit., p. 7.

40. Bord, op. cit., pp. 159–61.

41. Dr G. V. Robins, 'Earth Currents: The Possible Influence of Quartz', *The Ley Hunter*, no. 75, pp. 3–4.

42. See the chronological list of 500 cases given as an appendix in Alan Gauld and A. D. Cornell, *Poltergeists* (London: Routledge & Kegan Paul, 1979), which book is a thorough study of the phenomenon.

43. Guy Lyon Playfair, *This House is Haunted* (London: Souvenir Press, 1980).

44. PK and poltergeists are described in Nona Coxhead, *Mindpower* (London: William Heinemann, 1976; USA: St Martin's Press, 1977; London: Penguin Books, 1979) pp. 38–54 Penguin edn; Professor John Taylor's PK experiments with children are described in his book *Superminds* (London: Macmillan, 1975; London: Picador Books, 1976); and the Canadian experiment is fully detailed in Iris M. Owen with Margaret Sparrow, *Conjuring up Philip* (Canada: Fitzhenry & Whiteside, 1976; Ontario: PaperJacks, 1977).

45. For details of experiments see Peter Tompkins and Christopher Bird, *The Secret Life of Plants* (London: Allen Lane, 1974) and Jeffrey Goodman, *The Earthquake Generation* (London: Turnstone Books, 1979) ch. 9 and appendix.

46. Robins, 'The Dragon Awakes', op. cit., p. 6.

47. Eliade, *Patterns in Comparative Religion*, p. 154. The whole of Chapter 4 deals with 'The Moon and its Mystique'.

48. See Guy Lyon Playfair and Scott Hill, *The Cycles of Heaven* (London: Souvenir Press, 1978; London: Pan Books, 1979) pp. 243–6, Pan edn, for more details.

49. Maria Thun, *Work on the Land and the Constellations* (East Grinstead: The Lanthorn Press, 1977) p. 2.

50. See Eliade, op. cit., pp. 164–71.

51. See ch. 3, '"A Strange and Monstrous Serpent . . ."'.

52. The theory is fully set out in Dames, *The Avebury Cycle*.

53. See Colin Bloy's letter in *The Ley Hunter* no. 85 (1979) pp. 27–8; and Graves, *Needles of Stone*, pp. 41–2, 172–4.

54. Bob Stewart, *Where is Saint George?* Pagan Imagery in English Folksong (Bradford-on-Avon: Moonraker Press, 1977) p. 111.

Index